# Salvation for a Doomed Zoomie

### A TRUE STORY

# Salvation for a Doomed Zoomie

### A TRUE STORY

## John Galvin
### With Frank Allnutt

*Foreword by Gov. Joe Foss*

ALLNUTT PUBLISHING
INDIAN HILLS, COLORADO

Grateful acknowledgment is made to the estate of the late Vice Admiral Charles A. Lockwood, USN(ret.) for permission to reprint excerpts from *Through Hell and Deep Water*, by Admiral Lockwood and Colonel Hans Christian Adamson, USAF (ret.). Originally published by Greenberg Publishers, New York, 1956. Copyright © 1956 by Vice Admiral Charles A. Lockwood.

Published by

Allnutt Publishing
P.O. Box 247
Indian Hills CO 80454
(303) 697-0457

Library of Congress Catalog Card Number: 83-70694
ISBN 0-934374-01-5

Printed in the United States of America.

*To Susie*

# Acknowledgments

The author wishes to publicly acknowledge and thank the following people for their valuable contributions in helping to bring this book into existence:

**Gov. Joe Foss**, for his friendship, wise counsel and the compliment of writing the book's foreword.

**Capt. Frank Lynch**, USN (ret.), former executive officer of the U.S.S. *Harder* for providing me with a copy of the *Harder's* log ten years ago, reviewing the manuscript and making valuable clarification and corrections.

**Admiral John Coye**, USN (ret.), and former submarine commander, for reviewing the manuscript and making valuable corrections and suggestions dealing with submarines.

**Barrett Tillman**, author of numerous books and magazine articles on aviation, for his contribution of technical information about American and Japanese aircraft in World War II.

**Capt. James Rothermel**, USN (ret.), for his advice and counsel.

**John** and **Myrna Woudenberg**, for their editorial review of the manuscript and helpful suggestions.

**Susan Manor** and **Don Peterson** for editing the final manuscript.

**Frank Allnutt,** who gave me the vision to tell my story in book form; for his countless hours at a word processor, translating my notes and cassette recordings into manuscript form; and for publishing the book.

**Susie,** my wife, without whose understanding, love and encouragement this book could not have been written.

To these I extend my warmest gratitude for their assistance. Any omissions or factual inaccuracies in this book should not reflect on them, but are the sole responsibility of the authors.

John  Galvin

# Contents

# Foreword

It is a distinct honor and pleasure for me to have been asked to write the foreword to this book about my good friend John Galvin, with whom I share much in common.

John was a Navy Hellcat pilot in the Pacific during World War II and I was a Marine Wildcat pilot. We both know what it's like to be shot down and drink too much seawater while praying to be rescued. We have both been saved in numerous close calls with death. And we also share a deep spiritual bond.

This book is really three stories in one. It's about one of the most daring sea rescues of World War II...wild adventures on the legendary submarine *Harder*...and a man's lifetime search for meaning and purpose which he finally discovers, only to embark on life's *greatest* adventure.

The true story of John Galvin's amazing rescue has been previously told—in part—in numerous newspaper and magazine articles, books and on television. His is a story so fantastic that scarcely anyone would believe it were it not for official Navy documentation: the log of the U.S.S. *Harder*; photos taken by the Air Group Commander; the Navy's *Information Bulletin* magazine and its popular "Silent Service" submarine television series; the authoritative books, *Through Hell and Deep Water* and *Zoomies, Subs and Zeroes* by Admiral Charles W. Lockwood (former Commander, Submarines, Pacific Fleet) and Hans Christian Adamson; Frank Lynch, former exec on the *Harder*; and the men John flew with.

Mention of the *Harder* or its captain, Sam Dealey, to submariners brings a response of deep admiration and respect—almost reverence—because of the exploits of that sub and its courageous skipper and crew. Now, for the first time in print, John Galvin gives an eye-witness account of his suspenseful thirty-three day adventure on the *Harder* and the skipper who befriended him.

John Galvin's book is also the story of one man's spiritual quest to find meaning and fulfillment in life. For years he analyzed his many close brushes with death—as well as his personal successes and failures, in an attempt to discover a deeper purpose for living. But it wasn't until he met and married Susie—who was also searching—that his questioning heart finally discovered the right answers.

The action begins on page one, right in the cockpit of a screaming Hellcat, somewhere in the South Pacific during World War II. So fasten your seatbelt and hold on, because you are in for an unforgettable experience...one that just might launch you into the greatest personal adventure of your life!

Joe Foss

# Preface

I awoke with a start and sat bolt upright in bed. My breathing was deep and rapid, and I wiped beads of perspiration from my brow.

"What is it?" murmured my half-awake wife.

"I've got to tell my story, Susie—it's time *now* to tell the *whole* story."

She rolled over to face me and listened.

"I was dreaming and I heard a voice say, 'John, get up! Go tell your story. . .the time has come.'"

We talked for several minutes, then settled back. I was wide awake for awhile longer and retraced in my thoughts the incredible events that had taken place in my life and the history that I had seen in the making.

Over the years, legends have sprung from those experiences and men have told and retold bits and pieces of the stories. But I've steadfastly remained silent—for a couple of reasons.

You see, I wasn't a hero like Joe Foss—the Marine's top fighter ace who became a general, a governor, football commissioner and television personality. Quite the contrary; I did a very foolish thing and made a really impulsive blunder.

There was a time during the war when I thought for sure I was one doomed zoomie (as submariners call pilots). But salvation did come, and for years afterwards I was haunted by the possibility that my survival at sea and subsequent rescue were more than coincidence—but if that were true, then who? Why me? And for what purpose?

There is symbolism in this—a cliche perhaps, but nonetheless true: for many years following the war, I drifted aimlessly through life—sometimes on smooth seas and other times in troubled waters, struggling to survive with my priorities and purposes out of balance.

I can tell the whole story now, because what was missing has been found—and I want to share this great discovery with you. So if sometimes you feel adrift in life, it is my prayer that the message of this book will help lead to your rescue.

John Galvin

# Salvation for a Doomed Zoomie

A TRUE
STORY

# 1

# April Fool

In a screaming dive, plunging straight down out of the heavens like some wrathful Greek god, I am in command of the most awesome flying instrument of war yet devised by man. Spewing forth a fiery shower of sudden death from its wings, this terrifying creature nestles under its belly a sinister projectile, eager for release into a whistling trajectory that will imminently transform an unsuspecting target into an exploding inferno of death and devastation.

The angry fighter, cold and steel-hearted, is forebodingly named Hellcat. It is a 13,000 pound appellation of impending death—a Second World War aircraft, shrieking wildly in a furious attack on its prey, vehemently unleashing its lethal load. The Hellcat is an extension of my arms and legs—as if it and myself are one....

Hey, wait a minute! That might be the Hollywood stereotype of a blazing guns fighter pilot, but I'm not like that. I'm not some Greek god, I'm a mortal man—and a bit of a mouse-hearted one at that. I'm tense and apprehensive—a bundle of raw-edged nerves. I grit my teeth, and my flight suit is soaked beneath the arms. My gloved hands hide white knuckles that are locked in a vice-like grip on the joystick.

The date is April 1, 1944—April Fool's Day, a day whose namesake I will exemplify, a day that will mock me for years to come.

This was to have been a day of rest after two grueling but fascinating days of air combat over the Palau Islands in the southwest Pacific. But the Navy had other plans, and the early morning alarm for General Quarters clanged throughout the aircraft carrier, changing not only the course of the day, but the direction of my life.

*Bong-bong-bong....*

*"All hands! General Quarters!"*

The alarm startled me out of my sleep.

*"Now hear this,"* clamored the familiar but impersonal voice over the squawkbox. *"All hands! General Quarters! Man your battle stations."*

*Bong-bong-bong....*

Sleepy-eyed, I squinted at my watch. *Only three o'clock?* I muttered a groan. But General Quarters meant: "Move it— fast!" *What's up? Is the carrier under attack? Or will my squadron scramble into the air for another mission?*

The tart remembrance of aerial combat burst forth in my senses and triggered a release of adrenalin—not unlike the way a lemon excites the salivary glands.

I sprang out of my bunk and hurriedly dressed. This couldn't be an April Fool's Day joke (the Navy didn't have that much sense of humor), and it wasn't a drill. It was the real thing.

I darted out of my compartment and quickly merged into the streaming rush of men who crowded the light green painted passageway through "officers country." At full speed everyone scrambled toward his assigned place. Mine was our squadron's ready room, two decks up.

General Quarters was a graphic portrayal of the survival of the fittest, where heavy-weights got through and the timid were trampled or jostled out of the way. The place was like a Manhattan subway station during rush hour. Guys were on the run in every which direction, and the clumping of their boots against echoing steel decks thundered in my ears. Some were clambering up ladders (stairs to the uninitiated), and others, against the current, were trying to sqeeze down. Steel chains on the ladders rattled steadily as the parade of men went up or down, and water-tight doors clanged shut and were dogged down to seal off compartments so the ship would stay afloat in event of being torpedoed or bombed. Here and there, blue dungaree-clad "telephone talkers" relayed status reports on their respective stations into microphones mounted on their oversized steel helmets.

I shoved and elbowed my way up several ladders to reach the Ready Room. Pilots were standing around talking and joking and donning their flight gear. It reminded me of a football team's locker room minutes before kickoff.

It was all so new and exciting that I scarcely believed I was actually there experiencing it. I was fresh out of flight training—Ensign John R. Galvin, U.S. Navy—and proud of it! My unit—Fighter Squadron Eight—had only recently come on board the aircraft carrier U.S.S. *Bunker Hill.*

In the past two days we had pounded the Japs on Palau Island with bombs and machine guns.

My first four combat hops—wow! It was intoxicating! And if I hadn't bucked heads with those near-sighted recruiters back in Chicago, I would have missed the whole war! But my persistence paid off, and there I was, piloting Grumman's hot new aircraft, the F6F Hellcat. *If Dad could only see me now!*

As I waited for the briefing to begin, I wondered if this day would be like the others. Talk about an experience! We had caught the Japs by complete surprise, and everything we shot at burned or blew up—planes, gas tanks, hangars. Japs, too, I guess. But I didn't think about killing—only the incredible display of flashing explosions—huge mushroom clouds of belching fire and smoke. It reminded me of when I was a kid back in Burlington, Iowa: this was the kind of fireworks show I always wanted for the Fouth of July, but couldn't afford.

Writing about this, almost forty years later, makes me smile, because I wasn't much more than a kid *then*, flying Hellcats. I was painfully naive, a tall, slim, blond-headed, twenty-two-year-old from the easy-going and conservative Midwest.

In the pre-dawn darkness of that long ago April Fool's Day, following a breakfast of steak and eggs, we flew off the deck of the *Bunker Hill.* Our mission was to pulverize Woleai Atoll, a group of small, tropical islands, the largest of which was a Japanese staging island between Truk and New Guinea.

We were organized into divisions of four airplanes each, with two sub-sections of two planes each. I was in Fighter Division Seven, led by Division Leader Lt. Harlan I. Gustafson, Jr., a six-foot-four All American end from the University of Pennsylvania, and a native of nearby Norristown. In our other section were Ensign T.I. Brown of Lubbock, Texas and Ensign Chris Allen of Freeport, Texas.

Gus had considerable flying experience—was an instructor once. He was like a mother hen to the three of us ensigns. He jabbed his finger in our chests and drummed into our heads that the only way we'd make it through the war was to stay together when we flew combat.

"Yeah, yeah, we know all that," we'd tell him with youthful arrogance.

Gus came on strong as being tough (which he was), but inside, he was really a softy, and we took advantage of it. For example, he had a lisp that drew good-natured mimicking. He'd tell us something about combat flying, and someone

Allan, Brown, Gustafson and Galvin, October 15, 1943.

would immitate his lisp by saying, "That tho?" I always had to bite the side of my mouth to keep a straight face.

T.I. Brown was probably my best friend. He'd been my bunkie at Pongo and Norfolk, Virginia, and Alameda, California. Scrawny and hungry-looking, he stood six-one and had a pock-marked face, which wrongly characterized him as a thug to some. The image was perpetrated by his gusto for beer and his chain-smoking. Between cigarettes and many pet peeves, he was a nervous guy who carried a rabbit's foot for good-luck. When he drank (which was whenever he could), he had a propensity for losing his clothes and getting rolled.

My being so straight-laced always bothered T.I. Once, while on liberty together, he got fed up with me and said, "John, you're so damned holy, why don't you have a bottle of beer and be one of the guys? You just sit over there with that smirk on your face!"

I probably did smirk a little in disgust over T.I.'s heavy drinking because I never drank much. In fact, I didn't have my first beer until I went to flight training at Naval Air Station Glenview, Illinois (and the beer went right to my head). About the only drinking I did after that was to indulge in a ceremonial beer or brandy on board the carrier, which was a special privilege given only to pilots.

So, because I was something of a teetotaler, whenever T.I. and I hit the beach together he asked me to look out for him. One time, when I *wasn't* with him, he woke up on the botton of a dry swimming pool with only his shorts on. To this day he doesn't remember what happened, and we all teased him about going for a swim in a dry pool.

T.I., like all Texans, was proud of his state. His favorite boast was that his hometown of Lubbock was "the hub of the West and the home of Texas Tech."

Chris, on the other hand, projected totally the opposite personality. He was blond-haired and baby-faced, with a winning smile and easy-going disposition that made him popular with the guys. But he was no push-over: behind the controls of a Hellcat he was a real terror to the Japs.

So those were the other three guys in my division—Gus, T.I. and Chris. Great guys—like most of the men in our squadron.

Of course we had a few *prima donnas*—the ones who wanted to go off alone and win the war single-handed. Their kind usually got shipped home in a pine box, because they never learned to be team members or to respect the Japanese Zero for the superb fighter aircraft it was.

Maybe they made the error of believing—like most of the Europeans—that the Zero was a second-rate fighter and the Japanese were second-rate pilots. Such notions were far from accurate. While the Zero had some fatal drawbacks, it could outclimb and outmaneuver any American fighter. It was true that we Americans were better trained than the Japanese, but we were repeatedly cautioned never to underestimate the ability of the enemy to shoot you out of the sky!

"Don't take on a Zero one-on-one," Gus warned us over and over. "Don't be a sucker for a decoy. Don't go after what appears to be a straggler or a wounded duck, because they probably have some friends hiding in the clouds."

Instead, the emerging tactic (credited to Jimmy Thach, then brought to us in more sophisticated form by Scott McCuskey) was *team work*—stick together, cover each other, group tactics. *Never* leave your wingman or section leader to go after a target alone.

*Yeah, yeah, so much for basics*, was my sophomoric attitude. *We're out of flight training, now, let's go get the Japs!*

We had been in the air for a couple of hours when Woleai appeared in the distance—a thin sliver that broke the smooth, slightly curving symmetry of the far horizon.

## Salvation for a Doomed Zoomie

We flew in high over the atoll at 25,000 feet, and Gus gave us the close-up signal. We brought our Hellcats into a tight diving attack formation, to within ten feet of each other.

With Gus in front, we peeled and started to dive at the earth at full throttle. I prepared my Hellcat for the attack: arm machine guns...arm bomb...activate gunsight...switch on emergency fuel pump...turn on cockpit heater (to prevent cabin fogging in the dive through the warm, moist equatorial atmosphere). Last of all I pulled down my goggles—as protection against flying glass if I should get hit.

Dive! Dive! Down I went from that dizzy height, engine roaring, and wind screaming past the cockpit as airspeed picked up to 450 knots. What a sensation! Handling the controls of a Hellcat in a dive gives you an incredible, surging feeling of *power.*

Down I hurtled, not knowing what to expect. *What's waiting for us? Will anyone die?* Not *me*—but somebody else will. They always did. Maybe a dive bomber or torpedo bomber would get it—but not me.

No time to dwell on that now. The airfield was below, with its buildings, planes, vehicles and supply dumps. I squinted through my gunsight and saw some Jap planes parked in random little enclaves hacked out of the dense jungle at the edge of the airstrip. I eyed my altimeter: the needle was just dropping past the 5000 feet gradient. I squeezed the trigger on the front of the joy-stick, and all six machine guns blasted away, sending the Hellcat into a shuddering convulsion and filling my oxygen mask with the burned powder smell from dispatched bullets. I looked out the sides of the cockpit and watched the fire-breathing muzzles (collectively pumping out seventy-two rounds a second). My eyes followed the shower of bullets downward until they struck, ripping and exploding the targets to burning shreds. I turned my eyes to the altimeter, and at precisely 3500 feet, pressed the "Pickle"—the bomb button on top of the stick.

Like a blazing guns pilot in a low budget Hollywood production, I shouted "Bombs away! Here it comes, Jappers—a kiss of death!"

I pulled back on the stick and brought the Hellcat out of the steep dive. Gravity made the weight of my body sink into the seat. At the same time, I felt the air bladders of my skin-tight anti-gravity "Zoot Suit" gently squeeze around my legs and stomach—otherwise blood would rush from my head to my legs, causing me to black out.

Now I was flying parallel to the ground at no more than fifty feet off the deck. I glanced back over my shoulder and saw the bombs exploding into boiling clouds of fire and smoke.

"Bullseye!"

Then, my eyes were drawn to something off to the right. *A Japanese Betty bomber!* And it was parked all alone on the end of the strip. *A sitting duck!* A gleeful grin spread across my face. I was tempted beyond reason.

*I'll go for it!*

I rolled the Hellcat to the right, unconsciously and stupidly leaving Gus alone. But T.I. and Chris, who were on my right, had no choice but to follow me—or crash into my Hellcat. Then they too saw the bomber.

We all opened fire at the same time. Our bullets shattered the bomber, tearing into it and shredding its wings and fuselage, hurtling chunks into the air. Then the Mitsubishi exploded in a brilliant flash right before our eyes.

Our three Hellcats swooped in low to fly over the striken bomber. *What's that beyond it? Oh, no!* A chill froze my spine. There—just beyond the burning plane—was an ack-ack emplacement. The Jap gunners were firing a fusillade of 20-mm tracers at me—invisible until they whizzed past my cockpit. And I was flying right down the barrel of their guns!

*They can't miss!* I was nearly frozen with panic.

*Clumph. Clumph.*

My Hellcat shuddered.

## Salvation for a Doomed Zoomie

*They got me!*

T.I. and Chris, right behind me, saw it all, but were unscathed because the Japs were concentrating on the lead plane—*me!*

I quickly took stock of the situation. I wasn't hurt. The engine was running okay, and the plane was still in one piece—or so it seemed.

Through my oxygen mask I smelled the unmistakable acrid smoke of burned gun powder. I quickly glanced over the surface of the plane. The right wing! It looked as if someone had gone after it with a giant can-opener. The exploding shells had shredded my wing to ribbons, exposing some of its ribs.

But those trigger-happy Nips with the ack-ack guns weren't content with that—they were still pelting me with bullets in an attempt to knock me out of the sky.

Instinctively, I dived as close to the ground as possible and started jinking—making rapid, frantic, short turns right and left—in an effort to dodge the shower of deadly shells.

A few seconds went by and I was out of range of the guns and over the water. *No more love messages*, I thought sardonically, not seeing anymore tracers flying past. *Stay low*, I told myself, *and get outta here!*

*"John Remarkable,"* you've really done it now, I chided myself. I had just turned stupidity into disaster. *This is it. This is where I check out. It's the end of the world for me.* I could already smell eternity.

T.I. and Chris were still with me. They closed in tight on either side and a little behind. Over the crackling and popping of static in my earphones, I heard Gus hollering, realizing he was all alone: "Join up! Join up!"

"Hey, Gal," screamed T.I. over my earphones, "you're on fire, here on the right side!"

*Fire!* Fear shot through my senses and gripped my heart.

"That's nothin', you've got a cute little bonfire going over here on the left side, too, Dumbo," drawled Chris, using my nickname, which he always did.

Both my wing tanks were burning furiously. I can't remember ever feeling such panic! I broke out in a sweat, and tiny rivulets ran into my stinging eyes, blurring my vision. My heart was pounding so rapidly it felt like it was going to explode. *Now what do I do?* A million thoughts bombarded my brain.

*Jump!* Was my first impulse. *No, stay with the plane. Maybe the fire will blow out. But what if it doesn't?*

I kept going back and forth, arguing with myself. What a time to be so indecisive!

Precious seconds ticked away. Time was running out—fast!

I was zooming a scant ten feet above the water at full throttle, still doing upward of 300 miles an hour from the momentum of the dive. I pulled back on the stick to climb, just in case I would have to bail out.

*What's that?* I looked down at the floor. A little smoke was swirling up. Suddenly it gave way to a cloud of black smoke that gushed up into the cockpit and enveloped me in a burning cloud.

I started choking and frantically gasped for air. At any moment I expected to feel the flames searing my skin! Or else the plane would blow-up! If I didn't bail out soon, I'd be baptized in fire.

*Get out! Get out!* I thought, choked with panic. I rolled open the canopy hatch and the rushing wind fanned the fire into a fury. Angry red flames licked at my legs. I was a little more than 300 feet off the water—no time to slow down, and far below the recommended minimum altitude of 1500 feet to roll over on my back to bail out. But I had to get away from the fire!

It was a fight against the strong windblast just to get my head and shoulders and one arm out of the cockpit. But something was holding me back! *I'm stuck!* I kicked and kicked, but couldn't get free. Then I saw the problem: my G-Suit and radio cord were still connected. I forgot to unhook them and they were tethering me to the plane. The cockpit was engulfed in flames, but I had to go back inside and disconnect myself or else stay with the plane until it exploded or crashed.

With searing flames licking my oxygen mask and goggles, I somehow wriggled back into the cockpit and frantically disconnected the radio and oxygen lines and the zoot suit.

I wasted no time in climbing out again! The top of my body cleared the canopy and the blast of the 300-mile-per-hour wind *raked* me out. I flew back and slammed hard against the plane's tail, then went spinning off into oblivion.

# 2
# Doomed Zoomie

It seemed as though I was unconscious for a long time, but it could only have been seconds. Still stunned from hitting the tail of the plane, I knew I was falling and that I was going to land in the sea.

I desperately grabbed at the D-ring of my rip cord and gave it a yank—it slipped right out, but too easily. Something wasn't right! Normally it takes a healthy tug on the D-ring to break the string safety-tie and pull the pins out of their grommets. Parachutes are designed this way to prevent an accidental opening from a snag.

I mustered up the courage to look up. *The chute's open! Lucky me!* It must have popped open when I hit the tail. After that it was all automatic: bungees pulled back the container flaps; the spring-loaded pilot chute jumped out, caught the air, and pulled out the main canopy, which inflated quickly in the 300-mile-per-hour airstream.

I had no time to dwell on such things, because I was about to get a taste of the peril all pilots dread—landing in rough seas with a chute still on and being dragged.

Now, it's taken some time to read about the details, but in actuality, the whole episode took place in seconds—in the brief span of time it took for only one pendulum swing of the parachute.

*Wham!* I slammed into the water, face first. That water wasn't soft, and landing in it gave me the kind of jolt I'd expect from hitting the *ground*.

Everything happened so fast in the air that I didn't have time to sit back in the swing seat of the harness and unsnap the leg straps and chest strap (which is training manual procedure for a water landing). So now I faced the problem of getting out of the harness, and I mean *problem!* The sea was in one of its angrier moods, and because of the twenty-knot surface wind, the chute wouldn't collapse. I was in for a thrill that made Coney Island's roller-coaster look like a kiddie ride!

The chute dragged me through the rough sea and strong current, crashing me into fifteen-foot waves with the sensation of hitting the side of a brick building! The water was being driven into my face with such force that I couldn't suck in a breath. I was dragged under, only to have the chute jerk me out and back into the air again. Then I slammed into another wave, and the whole cycle repeated itself, over and over and *over!*

I was no match for Mother Nature's powerful forces of wind and water. The pull on the chute by the wind made it impossible to undo the leg and chest straps of the harness. I was completely helpless, *terrified!* I'd be airborne for a second, then brace just as I banged into another wave. Next I'd be underwater, choking, gasping, wondering if I'd ever see daylight again.

"Jesus!" I cried outloud, with no hint of an oath. If He could rebuke the waves once, couldn't He do it again?

## Salvation for a Doomed Zoomie

I must have vomited *gallons* of seawater.

More of this and I wouldn't be much more than low-grade shark bait!

Running the gauntlet at the business end of that chute was a fast ticket to nowhere, and one joy-ride I could do without. But I couldn't unbuckle the harness. ("The tighter the better," the parachute riggers told us in survival training.) I tried to collapse the chute by pulling on one of the belted risers that attached my harness to the shroud lines. But because it was straining tightly in the strong wind, that was impossible.

*The frog-sticker!*—my survival knife! Razor-sharp! I pulled it from the sheath strapped on my lower right leg and started hacking away through the riser's heavy webbing.

Only a few strands left, then...*snap!* With a fourth of the shroud lines cut loose, air started spilling out of the canopy, and the mass of flimsy silk collapsed onto the water.

The thrill-ride was over!

But my problems were not.

I started sinking like a rock! And no wonder, I was weighted down with a bandolier of ammo, machete, 45- automatic, and my water-logged flight jacket and zoot suit. But I got the harness off and managed to pull the toggles to crack the two $CO_2$ cartridges on my Mae West life jacket.

*Oh, no!* All it did was fizz and bubble! The air was escaping from a gaping tear on the right side. *Must have happened when I hit the tail.* I cussed just to be cussing.

I can't begin to tell you how discouraging... how *utterly* discouraging this can be to a floundering half-swimmer in such a predicament. Long before however, the Navy Department had thought the whole thing through about ditching at sea, and had a back-up plan. Included in my bag of survival tricks was an inflatable rubber life raft. I wrestled the raft free of its container with all the excitement of a kid opening a Christmas present, and frantically pulled the toggle on the $CO_2$ bottle.

Let's hear it for the Navy! (Dad always told me the Navy was the best branch of the military.) I just stared wide-eyed, waiting for the raft to inflate.

*What the*—? To my horror the air rushed out through a deep gash in the rubber!

My heart sank. I threw up again.

I couldn't believe I could get myself into such a jam. What was I doing out here anyway? Why wasn't I back home in Burlington, pushing a lawnmower around Charlie's yard? It really was ironic. I mean, it wasn't as though I had been drafted. *I just* had *to join the Navy and see the world, didn't I?*

But forget that: I was down to two options—sink or swim! *Sink?* There were hundreds—if not thousands—of feet of dark, threatening water beneath me. I'd drown! I was *horrified* at the thought of sinking into that deep, dark water. I never took to water all that well and didn't even like being on the *surface!* The remaining option was to swim. *Great! Just great!* Only weeks earlier I had flunked the Navy swim test!

Swell choices!

*Well, John Remarkable, why didn't you take swim lessons like your Mom told you?* I could have kicked myself.

No time like the present to learn. Kick and paddle, that's what I'd have to do. But as soon as I tried to draw my right arm out of the water for a stroke I felt a stabbing pain—like electricity shooting through my entire right side. Now, worse than the pain, was the frightening realization that *my right arm and right leg were almost useless!*

Panic gripped me again. *I'm going to drown! There's nobody to help me!*

"Please, God, please help me!" I cried out loud.

For all my trouble I just got another mouthful of saltwater. The roiling in the pit of my stomach could not be ignored, and I heaved again. Vomit and saltwater—yuck! But worse than that was the rancid taste of fear.

*Get hold of yourself,* I thought, a little upset with the way I let panic overtake me. I knew I had to discipline my senses. *Just calm down and think. No more arguing with yourself. Analyze the situation, okay? Okay. So what should I do first? Get those heavy field shoes off!*

*That's it!* I complimented myself. *Now you're getting back in control of things.*

I reached down to untie my shoes—but under I went again. I fought back to the surface, coughing and sputtering seawater. There went my control.

I tried again—and again and *again.* I guess in my excitement I pulled the loops of the laces into knots. I was getting more and more exhausted, and being able to use only one arm and one leg, I decided I'd best use my strength to stay afloat.

I had to shed some weight. The .45—chuck it. The bandolier—take it off. The machete—it goes too.

What an effort! My strength was going, fast.

*If only I could get some rest.*

In desperation, I tried paddling on my back, using my good left arm and left leg. It was a Herculean effort that produced only feeble results. But it kept my head above water! I ventured to take a deep breath—but it was ill-timed, because at that precise moment a wave broke over my face. I went into another spasm of coughing, gasping and vomiting. I was losing strength. *How much longer can I hold out?*

I regained my composure, and, at the top of a crest, rolled over on my stomach long enough to get some bearings. I caught a glimpse of the distant island and the fringe of palm trees—*miles away!* (five miles, I learned later).

It was too far.

*I'm done for! I'm going to drown! No help! No* Mae West! *No life raft!*

What else could I do?

*The zoot suit—get out of that coffin!* ("The tighter your G-suit, the less likelihood of losing consciousness when pulling out of a dive,'' the training manual had advised.) But by now the water had thoroughly soaked the heavy corded material and it had shrunk so tightly that I couldn't loosen any of the zippers. And because there were no check valves, water flowed freely through the air-hose, filling the bladders!

What a helpless predicament. Wasn't *anyone* interested in my destiny? Where was that lifeguard submarine, anyway? And where was God? Had He forsaken me too? I felt like Christ on the cross. *Please, God, don't let me drown. Please!*

Then I realized that God wasn't going to let me *drown.* Because just then I saw it—the first *fin!*

*Oh my God! Eaten by a shark! Is this how I'm going to check out?*

Things went from bad to worse; my hungry visitor wasn't alone. I spotted two more sharks—then six or seven circling me. I was almost hysterical.

*Calm down! Now don't panic,* I tried to get hold of myself. Then I remembered the dye marker. Boy, did I tear open those bags in a jiffy. I had all six of them open as fast as I could (I carried extras), all the while turning my body around to see if a shark was sneaking up on me from the rear. I must have released enough dye to color half the Pacific brilliant green.

What does this have to do with sharks? I'll explain. Primarily, dye marker is intended to be used by pilots downed at sea for easy spotting by search aircraft. *And,* according to the Navy Survival Manual: "Sharks might not swim into the cloud caused by the dye."

Not that I had so much confidence in the survival manual, it's just that I was willing to try *anything* to keep those razor-mouthed sharks at a distance!

Waiting apprehensively, I watched the dye spread out in the water around me, fully expecting an arm or leg to be bitten off. (I paddled with short strokes!) But not a single shark penetrated that circle of dye! Evidentally they had gone... fear kept gnawing away at me.

I felt a little ashamed over the bad things I had thought about the guy who wrote the survival manual (and his mother).

After several minutes the cloud of dye dissipated in the rough sea. It was a miracle the sharks didn't get me. And I don't say that lightly.

How long did all this take? I don't know. I didn't have a good recollection of the passing of time. I mean, you just aren't at your best when you're drowning and fighting off sharks. Even after things quieted down I'd swim for what seemed like half an hour, only to check my government-issued waterproof watch, and see that a scant five minutes had elapsed.

I just remember the chilling, inexorable hopelessness that overwhelmed me. More dreaded than the unseen, circling sharks, fear haunted me like an unwelcome ghost lurking in the ocean's depths. Never before had I felt so forlorn. I was trapped. Done for. In the middle of the Pacific with no one to help me. I felt that fate was cheating me out of living a full life. I must have drifted off into a dreamlike period of suspension, and strange thoughts came to mind.

Would my body ever be recovered? Not likely. How would my parents find out? I could just see a couple of ash-faced Navy officers walking up to the front door of their house. There's a knock on the door. Mom and Dad answer, their faces apprehensive with concerned, quizzical expressions. In a somber tone, one of the Navy officers says, "Mr. and Mrs. Galvin, I'm afraid we have some sad news for you...."

And the epitaph on my tombstone—what will it read? *Here lies John R. Galvin, an April Fool who broke the rules—and never should have been a Navy pilot in the first place.*

A wave slapped me back to reality.

*I'm going to drown!*

It was like a voice that I heard over and over again: *Galvin, you're going to drown.* The thought kept gnawing away at me.

Then a strange euphoric feeling crept in, and I reasoned calmly and pragmatically that *Drowning is not so painful. It's a lot better than being eaten by sharks.*

*Ouch!* A cramp in my leg. The pain shocked me awake. No time to think about peacefully drowning; I had to massage away the cramp or I'd be in *real* trouble! I quit paddling so I could use my one good arm. Of course, I started to sink immediately. I rubbed my leg for a minute, then resumed treading water. I kept alternating like this until I got the muscle relaxed. Minutes later the cramp hit again. Back to the massage routine. This happened several times. When the cramp would go away, then my mind always grew numb and started playing tricks on me again.

*Drowning isn't so bad,* I'd almost convince myself, drifting dangerously close to unconsciousness. *It will all soon be over....*

I honestly believed that I was being disenfranchised from the world of the living. I had a strange fascination with knowing I was about to die. What great adventure lay ahead?—*if any!*

"Don't quit! Don't quit!" someone shouted.

It startled me out of my lethargy. Hey! That sounded like my *Dad's* voice! Was my mind playing tricks again? I started swimming like crazy.

Then the other voice (it was more a sinister thought) came back: *"You're going to drown!"*

Rest. I needed to rest.

The sinister thought returned. *"Just take a few gulps of water and it will all be over."* It was like the devil was luring me into the depths of Hell (though at the time I didn't believe there was a devil).

I snapped out of my stupor and started swimming like mad. This went on and on.

Then a very strange and remarkable thing happened: there was an invasion of brilliant light, and the water around me

37

took on the appearance of morguelike luminosity. Time seemed to stand still, and I was enraptured by this surrealistic experience. I heard a voice, calling: "John!"

*Who called me?* It wasn't Dad, and it wasn't the devil. It was a *third voice* and I didn't recognize it. It was like someone was knocking on the door to my mind. Could it be?...was God talking to me? Or was it all a dangerous distortion of reality?

Unaware of what was happening to me, I had slowly drifted beneath the surface, and now my brain was starved for oxygen, and my mind was behaving strangely. I was beginning to drown and didn't realize it.

The third voice jolted my mind into consciousness. Maybe it *wasn't* imagined.

*My God! I'm under the water!* My fear glands activated all over again.

I began thrashing toward the surface. *How far down am I?*

It seemed as though I would never reach air. My lungs were about to burst. *I have to breathe!*

Then I broke through the surface and sucked spasmodically for air. Coughing and gurgling, I looked around to see who had called my name. But there was no one to be seen.

I was hardly aware of an approaching wave. It made no difference. Crippled and numb with pain, I could no longer muster the strength to brace for it. It smacked into me with a whallop and tossed me around like a cork. The salt water burned my eyes and nose and lungs. (Doctors have since told me that I must have been dehydrating rapidly.)

I was at the mercy of the sea. This was it: I could hang on no longer. My time had run out. Then....

*Thump!* I was aroused by a vicious crack on the head.

*What am I doing on the bottom? Is this heaven? Or hell?*

There was pain in my lungs...I had to *breathe!*

Instinctively, with a final spurt of energy, I desperately kicked for the surface. But my feet *jabbed into something solid* and my head and shoulders broke the surface.

I was standing in shallow water! Just then another wave came crashing down and pounded me against a coral head. I grabbed for the outjutting and clung to safety.

*Ouch!* The razor-sharp coral cut my hands painfully; I wouldn't be able to hang on for long. But I was exhausted and hurting too badly to let go and battle the rough breakers.

I caught my breath and regained some strength. Blinking salt water from my burning, swollen eyes, I looked around. I was inside the reef, and between me and the beach were 500 yards of fifteen-foot breakers and treacherous riptides.

"I made it!" I tried to shout, my voice raspy and weak.

My Mae West was useless so I took it off, then started stumbling, wading and paddling toward the beach.

The waves pummeled me mercilessly, and I rolled head over heels, scraping against the bottom's abrasive coral. Staggering and falling in the knee-deep water, I used my good left elbow to crawl like a crab, and eventually reached the shore's edge.

I pulled myself up onto the sand, then passed out, my legs still dangling in the foamy surf. Somehow I had made it past the coral-encrusted barrier reef, and the tumbling surf carried me on to shore. My head was bleeding in several places, and my hands were shredded like bloody hamburger from the coral. It had taken four and a half hours to reach shore.

The odds were greatly against being rescued. What was one pilot to the mission of the Fifth Fleet? Was my life worth the risk of attempting a rescue?

If my floatation equipment hadn't been damaged and I had remained in the water, one of our seaplanes or lifeguard submarines might have picked me up. But I was stranded on the beach.

Still stunned and racked with pain, I was the only American on a tiny island that was overrun with Japs who would soon hunt me down. Where could I go? Where could I hide? It made little difference at that moment, because I was too weak to move.

I had pleaded for God to deliver me from danger in the angry sea, but, now, lying on that deserted beach, did I think to thank Him? No, because it never occurred to me that it was the hand of God that had saved me. All I could think about was how to get rescued off that Japanese-held island. Pray again? It never crossed my mind. It was different when I was drowning, but now there was less urgency; I was *temporarily* safe.

It was nothing short of a miracle that I was alive on that beach...and it would take another miracle for me to get off. Instead of trusting God for salvation, I kept asking myself: *Where* is *that lifeguard submarine?*

# 3
# Formative Years

**H**ad Mom known the condition I was in on that beach, she would have prayed, believing that God would intervene with a miraculous rescue.

She was big on praying, read the Bible to us every night, and taught us kids the Lord's Prayer and the Twenty-Third Psalm—*The Lord is my Shepherd*....

"If you are ever in trouble or need help," she would tell us, "Pray to God, believing that He will help you, and He will. He will hear you and answer your prayers."

Those were the years of the Great Depression, a time of many hardships and discouragement that gave Mom plenty of opportunity to exercise her faith. And that was her attitude: what were seen by others as "impossible situations" were to her *opportunities* to trust God and grow in her faith.

Dad was a plumber, but back then there wasn't much work available, so we lived a humble lifestyle bordering on poverty. Though we had little in the way of material possessions,

Mom and Dad always looked at the positive side of things, and this helped us to grow close together as a family.

I had two sisters and a brother. Mary was older than I, and Helen was younger. My brother Marty, who was eighteen months older than me, contracted encephalitis when he was eleven.

His sickness was one more trial to test Mom's faith. But she was unwavering in her deep religious convictions, and my brother's poor health, instead of getting Mom down, only contributed to shaping her strong faith and godly character.

As the disease in Marty's frail body progressed, his need for physical therapy required Mom's constant attention. She massaged and exercised his fingers, hands and arms, toes, feet and legs several times a day in an effort to keep them from atrophying. It was strenuous, but she never complained. Though her effort was spent without seeing encouraging results, she never gave up hope.

The doctors at Mayo Clinic said Marty would soon die from the disease, but, undaunted, Mom never stopped praying and trusting God that he would be healed. Marty and all of us, particularly Mom, were richly blessed through those years— mostly in subtle spiritual and character-building ways. We were just happy that Marty was a part of our family for as long as he was. When Marty died just before turning twenty, we had much to be thankful for, and Mom never blamed God or got angry at Him for not healing her son.

Mom was a real saint, but sadly, all of us in the family— especially Dad—thought she was overly religious. I guess I developed the attitude that Christianity was only for troubled mothers! Though I pushed God to the back of my mind, I can't say I *completely* crossed off religion, because I remembered the Twenty-Third Psalm and often recalled it when the going got tough. Dad, though, was a downright religious skeptic.

He was a wiry little Irishman with an outgoing personality and a bent toward irreverence. He could really be boisterous at times, but usually only at home and among friends. Once in a while his irreverence would come out in his language in public, and this embarrassed Mom no end. When she remonstrated him for it, he always came up with his classic response: "If they don't like my quaint Irish ways, they can kiss my sweet Irish patootie!," which only elicited another disgusted look from Mom.

Dad was basically a good, moral person. He and Mom always taught us to be honest and upright, and to work hard. And they had a "don't list" as long as your arm: "Don't swear," "Don't smoke," "Don't mess around with girls," "Don't drink booze," and "Don't gamble." Had drugs been the problem then as it is now, I'm sure that would have been one more "don't."

One of the most important things I learned from Mom and Dad was to work hard at a respectable, honest job. I got my early training doing chores around the house, and by the age of twelve, I was ready to venture out into the business world.

My first job was shining shoes on a downtown street corner. Business was slow, because in those days you were lucky to *own* a new pair of shoes, let alone pay someone to *shine* them. Regardless, I thought the job paid okay. I earned seventy-five cents in a typical day, working from seven in the morning until ten at night. On a good Saturday I would make another thirty-five to forty cents in tips. When I got tipped that well, I'd have lunch at the White Spot Diner—two hamburgers, a glass of milk and a piece of hot apple pie. All for a *quarter*. What a banquet!

Mom insisted that I give a portion of my earnings to God: a dime in the Sunday School basket, another dime in the offering plate at church service, and a nickel for Epworth League on Sunday night.

We hardly ever missed Family Night suppers at church on Wednesday, and I always looked forward to going. To Mom it was the spiritual and social highlight of the week (and I think she thought we all felt that way, too). But to Dad it was an obligation. For me it was an opportunity to horse around with my friends and eat all I wanted. It also had some financial benefits; Mom didn't make me put any money in the collection plate.

The values Dad taught us were more on a temporal level. One thing he wouldn't stand for was cowardice. "Don't ever be a quitter," he used to admonish Marty and me (because we were always getting into fights at school or with the neighborhood bully). If we ever got badly beat up or ran from a fight, Dad would lecture us, then give us a paddling with a board. We dreaded him worse than the bullies.

Dad wasn't always a boisterous authoritarian; he had a soft side as well. It showed mostly when he was kidding Mother or spinning one of his yarns about his boyhood deviltry.

Whether I picked it up at home or at church I can't say, but I was blessed (or cursed) with a better than average tenor voice. When I got older, I sang in the choir at the First Methodist Church in Burlington.

Usually, I was the only tenor, but once in a while another guy would sit in. You should have heard him. If I sounded bad, he sounded like a cross between an overly tight violin string and someone screeching fingernails across a chalkboard! *Amazing Grace* was when he wasn't there.

I graduated from high school with little thought of going to college. Mom and Dad didn't have the money to send me, and there wasn't a job that paid enough for me to save what I'd need. But thanks to a man named Charlie Phelps, college became a reality. Charlie, a big, garrulous insurance broker, and his wife Florence, were such close friends of my family that they were almost relatives. I cut their grass regularly, so

I saw a lot of them. They had no children of their own, and Charlie took an uncle-like special interest in me.

One day, while taking a break from cutting Charlie's lawn, I sat with him in the shade and he started probing into my plans for the future. He was particularly interested in seeing me go to college. I told him that no one in my family had ever gone to college, so I hadn't given it much thought. Besides, I didn't think I could ever afford to go.

"You've *got* to go to college," he insisted.

"I don't think I'm smart enough."

"Listen, John, college is where you go to *become* smart. And haven't you ever heard of scholarships?"

"*Me,* get a scholarship?" I laughed. It sounded like a joke because my high school grades were just average.

Charlie was serious, though, and he did more than just encourage me; he volunteered to help. Within a few days he found out that the Methodist Church had a Student Loan Fellowship, and he helped me apply. To my surprise, I got a loan. And since Charlie was in the Masons and Knights Templar, he applied in my behalf to the organization's student foundation, which resulted in my receiving a small scholarship.

The loan and scholarship, coupled with whatever I earned at odd jobs, met my expenses in attending junior college in Burlington for two years. And Charlie even convinced me that my I.Q. would not keep me from getting a degree.

Charlie continued to be interested in my college education and shoved me in the direction of Northwestern University at Evanston, Illinois.

"As long as you are going to have to earn the money," he reasoned, "why not go to the best?

"And another thing," he cautioned, "don't come back to Burlington looking for a job, 'cause you won't find one. There aren't that many good jobs in a little town like this, and you don't know the right people to even get in for an interview."

At the time I was grateful to Charlie for what he was doing for me, but it wasn't until years later that I was mature enough to fully appreciate his friendship and help. How many young people have a friend and supporter like Charlie Phelps?

Attending Northwestern would be a juggling act: maintaining a B average to keep the scholarships, while working at odd jobs to pay for room and board.

Whether it was because I inherited my Mom and Dad's optimism or because I was a backwards, small-town kid, I don't know, but that fall, off I went to Northwestern, fully confident of completing my college education. I had two suitcases of clothes and thirty-five dollars to my name. I had made no provisions for a place to stay or for meals, naively assuming someone would take care of me! When I arrived, I walked with a confident bounce right up to the registrar's desk and announced with a grin: "Here I am!"

What a Rube!

# 4

# Call to Arms

It was a sunny, cold Sunday morning in Evanston, and the town was typically sleepy-quiet. Little did I know that it was the proverbial calm before the storm. That day would mark the end of the Depression era and the traumatically painful beginning of another—one of upheaval and uncertainty. It was December 7, 1941.

That year I was a senior at Northwestern University, weary of four years of round-the-clock studies and odd jobs that barely made ends meet. Dorm living and fraternity life were unaffordable, so I had settled for living in a mens' rooming house—a private home not far from campus.

The Christmas season was upon us, and downtown Evanston glistened with holiday lights and tinsel. The stores were decked out with traditional decorations of Santas, Christmas trees and nativity scenes. Familiar carols blared from loud-speakers mounted on lamp posts that protruded from the crowded sidewalks. Almost every corner had its own

## Salvation for a Doomed Zoomie

Salvation Army bell-ringer and large red kettle suspended from a tripod for collecting donations for the needy. And I was there too—right in the midst of it, tasting the merriment of the season as a member of the Northwestern men's quartet, strolling down Howard Street singing Christmas carols.

Though the Depression still lingered in the Midwest, people scraped together enough change to find some fantasy escape by going to the movies. It was the time of the Hollywood musical, the Barrymore family, Betty Grable, Jean Harlow and Clark Gable. Who could ever forget Judy Garland and "The Wizard of Oz"? Or the saga of "Gone With the Wind"?

Northwestern was a football power, and every guy I knew (myself included), dreamed of driving his date to a game in a new Oldsmobile or Studebaker or Packard.

Between studies and work, I had little spare time and no extra money for such pleasures. It was hard enough to find time for homework, which was why, on that particular Sunday morning, I was cramming for an engineering exam.

I made it a habit while studying not to listen to the radio or phonograph records. It wasn't that I didn't like music, because I did—very much. Glen Miller, Tommy Dorsey, I liked all the big bands. And I never tired of listening to Frank Sinatra or any of the name vocalists of the day. It was just that I could study better without the distraction.

Because the radio wasn't on, I did not hear the morning news programs or the reports out of the Pacific that stunned the nation. To me, that day was just another peaceful Sunday morning.

My love for music was mostly satisfied by singing tenor in the Northwestern *a cappella* choir, which practiced several days a week, including Sunday afternoons. I sang in the choir for practical reasons, too. I was majoring in engineering, but the only way I could get by financially was to accept yet a third

50

scholarship—a modest one that required membership in choir and a minor in vocal music.

That Sunday, time was getting away from me, as it always seemed to whenever I was studying. Choir practice was about to start, and I would have to run all the way across the quad to the music building, so as not to be late.

Rehearsal started in the usual way—a dozen conversations going at the same time, joking and laughing. The choir director, George Howerton, brought us to order and started our warm-up exercises. As we settled down to the serious business of singing, the outside world was quickly forgotten.

We were rehearsing when one of my classmates, Bill Peterman, burst into the choir room, interrupted us and breathlessly blurted out: "The Japanese have bombed Pearl Harbor!"

There were shocked expressions and stunned silence. Then, after a moment, everyone started talking at once.

"Where's Pearl Harbor?" asked one of the sopranos.

"In Hawaii," answered a bass.

No one seemed to know much about Pearl Harbor, but the news that the Japanese had the audacity to bomb an American military base was met with apprehension and anger.

I just kept my mouth shut and my ears open, because I had never heard much about Hawaii, except that America laid claim to the islands. Some of the other choir members were more knowledgeable, and minutes later, after I listened in on their conversations, the picture became clearer.

Later more details of the attack began to unfold. Pearl Harbor was the base for our Navy's Pacific Fleet. The Japanese navy had made a surprise attack that morning, while most of our military men were off duty—attending church, playing golf or tennis, sunning themselves on the beach, or just sleeping in. Our ships were sitting ducks, moored for the Jap predators, and many were sunk or heavily damaged. The loss of life was staggering—about 2500 according to preliminary reports.

President Franklin Roosevelt, in a somber nationwide radio address, called December 7 the "Day of Infamy," and announced that he was asking Congress for the authority to declare war against the Japanese Imperialist government.

The gloom over Pearl Harbor and the grim specter of war doused the Christmas spirit like a wet blanket.

All that fall I had been preoccupied with studies and had paid little attention to world events. Oh, I had caught snatches of news here and there about Hitler's aggression in Europe, but it seemed so far away that I never felt personally affected. I had no idea there was a Japanese threat to America, let alone that we were on the verge of war.

Now, after Pearl Harbor, I found myself listening more to radio news and reading the newspaper, trying to learn—literally—what in the world was going on.

Before Pearl Harbor the world seemed so big, but now it had grown smaller, with Germany and Japan all the closer to America, and therefore more threatening. I no longer felt detached from world events; I knew I was about to be drawn into the churning current of world conflict. To reiterate a cliche, destiny was knocking at my door.

I wasn't the only one who felt that way: the draft was on every young man's mind. Most college students were getting temporary deferments, but life after graduation was sure to be the military. Who knew what would come next, or when?

At that time, my own immaturity wasn't capable of bringing me much peace of mind, so I sought solace in remembering Dad's wise advice. Drawing on his Irish philosophy and plumber's pragmatism, he always said, "John, if a war ever comes along, join the Navy because it's a more gentlemanly branch of the service—cleaner and higher class. You always sleep in a clean bunk and have hot meals."

That's what Dad had *heard,* anyway. The truth was, he had never been in the service. At the time of World War I, he had two kids and was too old for military duty.

Most of what Dad knew about the military he picked up from his brother, my uncle Paul, who had been drafted into the Army in World War I. Uncle Paul used to fill Dad's head with all sorts of graphic war stories about trench fighting, rotten food, mutilated and bloated corpses, sleeping in the mud and snow, and the terrors of mustard gas. Yet there is some humor in this: Uncle Paul had never seen combat. He didn't even get close to the fighting area! His tales were hearsay, embellished with his vivid imagination, in short, just a lot of hot air!

We were in another world war now, and Germany was on the march again. Only this time, the Germans were led by a madman who was armed with modern weapons of death, and who was backed by the other Axis powers of fascist Italy and the Japanese imperialists.

News reports started filtering in from China and France and other exotic places where the war was being fought. There were sensational stories about the heroics of the Flying Tigers, the Royal Air Force and other fighting units, and they sounded adventuresome and romantic. Like any young man at the time, I dreamed dreams of grandeur, seeing myself in the role of a courageous fighting man—or better yet, a soldier of fortune. There is nothing like a war to give a young man the feeling of destiny's call.

While the war was the main topic of conversation on campus, and I was concerned about being drafted, I never said much about my feelings to anyone. I couldn't afford the cost of a long-distance telephone call to Mom and Dad, but I did write every week. I never mentioned the draft and neither did they, but I'm sure they were as concerned as I was.

My older sister Mary had already joined the WACs. I remember her half-joking remark just before she joined the WACs: "I'm not going to sit out the war in Burlington, Iowa, while all the guys go off to fight the war."

## Salvation for a Doomed Zoomie

My younger sister, Helen, right out of high school, married Bob Eisenhart who then joined the Marines.

Back in my senior year in high school, I had tried to persuade Mom to let me join the local Navy Reserve unit, but she wouldn't hear of it. Whether it was a mother's intuition or not I don't know, but it was a good thing I didn't join, because when the war broke, that unit was quickly activated, and most of its men got wiped out in the early stages of combat in the Aluetians.

And now I was faced with the draft. I didn't want to get drafted, but I felt that if I was called I would go without hesitation. Most of the guys I knew felt the same way. Some decided to wait for Uncle Sam's telegram, and others chose to join up voluntarily. I was having a hard time making up my mind, until....

Not too many days after Pearl Harbor, I heard a radio program promoting the glories and benefits of Naval Aviation. The Navy was advertising for pilots, promising: "Earn your Navy wings of gold" and a $500 a year bonus for anyone who would sign up.

Well, let me tell you, $500 was a *fortune* in those days! Keep in mind the Midwest was still in the clutches of the Great Depression, and there I was, studying my backside off hoping to graduate in June, getting further and further into debt in government student loans.

Also about that time, the Navy started a campus recruitment campaign at the Big Ten colleges to induce seniors to join the Navy and become aviators. The recruiters capitalized on school pride by tying in the school's nickname in the campaign. So, to those of us at Northwestern, they invited us to join up with the "Flying Wildcats." At Indiana, the program was called the "Flying Hoosiers," and at Notre Dame it was the "Flying Irishmen."

The strategy was to recruit forty to fifty students—particularly popular athletes and student leaders—and use their names as endorsement propaganda to get others to join.

54

I guess the plan was successful, because even *I* started thinking about joining. Having never been in an airplane, I didn't know if I would enjoy flying, but the life of a Navy pilot sounded adventuresome and fun. And besides, everyone was saying, "Sign up with the Navy or Marines—anything is better than waiting to get drafted into the Army." It only confirmed what I always heard Dad say.

I just couldn't get it out of my mind. Not that I was so patriotic, you understand, it was more for the adventure and the pay. I could become a Naval Aviator and also get that $500 yearly bonus to boot. I was hooked.

Right after the first of the year, I went down to the Chicago Board of Trade Building to sign up. The recruiters turned out to be some familiar athletes and student leaders from Chicago, and I was impressed that *they* had chosen the Navy, too. Dad was sure right about the Navy being the best!

I was given the various enlistment tests—mental, physical and apptitude—all of which were a breeze. Afterwards, I appeared before a selection committee for a personal interview. I remember the men's names very well, but to spare them embarrassment, I won't mention them here—except for Lincoln Maythem, an older fellow and former business man and administrator, who was sympathetic toward me and the only helpful one in the bunch. He even coached me along so I would come up with the right answers in the interview. The other recruiters included a Chicago socialite and former basketball star, as well as one who was a physician (he went on to become a flight surgeon at Glenview Naval Air Station, north of Chicago).

Well, this was an important interview, and I didn't want to muff it. I remembered Dad's advice for situations such as this: "Be a gentleman and address superiors as 'Yes, sir,' and 'No, sir.'"

The interview began with one of the men saying, "You know, you gotta be tough to be a Naval aviator."

*Can't disagree with that,* I thought.

"It takes a lot of stamina to fly an airplane," said another recruiter. "You know, war isn't a playground."

*Now, this is a strange way for them to be talking to me. I already know all that.*

Finally, one of them rose from his chair and said, "We'd like for you to wait out in the hall, Galvin, and we'll call you in a few minutes."

So I waited. An hour went by...then two hours. At last, near the end of the long, boring day, one of the recruiters came out and informed me almost curtly, "No soap, Galvin." That's *all* he said, then turned and walked briskly back into the room and closed the door.

*No soap!* I thought. At first I was confused, then angry, and then hurt. I got up and started out of the building, then noticed my file folder on a desk. I glanced down both ends of the nearly empty hallway and saw that no one was looking. I picked up the folder and opened it. There were the results of my tests. Just as I thought: I had passed them all.

Then my eyes caught a written evaluation of the interview: "We feel that this man, because of his involvement in the music school, is probably a temperamental and effeminate musician, not suitable for flying."

I stared at the report in total disbelief. *Effeminate? Temperamental?* Why I had *always* worked hard at what I considered to be "masculine" work. For the past two years, I had worked part time as a laborer, carrying heavy buckets of cement at construction sites. There was nothing effeminate about doing *that* job! I was *fuming!*

All the way back to the boarding house I kept mulling over the report, getting angrier by the minute. I knew that some musicians were effeminate, and I had heard stories about homosexuals in the entertainment business. But I didn't know of any at Northwestern. As for temperamental musicians, at college I had observed that musicians were temperamentally

56

more balanced than the average person. Later I learned why: musicians find an outlet for pent-up emotions through their music. But I had a mixed temperament, I guess, because while I was a musician, I wasn't going to just "sing away" my anger. If it was a fight the Navy wanted, then a fight I would give them!

I decided to talk over my predicament with Dr. William Gellerman, who taught my educational psychology course. He was a rough and tough guy who had been born and raised at an Oregon logging camp—and *talked* that way! Surely he could understand, and maybe help in some way.

After I told him my story, he said thoughtfully, "Well, John, I am a psychologist, you know, and I think I might be able to help you."

We talked a while longer, and Dr. Gellerman said, "You've got two strikes against you, John. First of all, you are enrolled in the music school, and there are a certain amount of effeminates and homosexuals in the field of music. The second strike is your hair—it's too long."

I started to protest, but he waved me to silence and continued: "Now, I know that long hair is the popular thing with college men these days, but it's strictly taboo with the military. To them it's effeminate."

I was too embarrassed to tell him that I only wore my hair long because I was self-conscious about my protruding ears.

He continued by saying it would help if I weren't "such a gentleman." He told me to "Use some four-letter words, and don't wear a neck-tie or scarf [scarves were a fad]. Don't say, 'Yes, sir,' or 'No, sir,' just 'yes' or 'no.'"

We ended our long talk, with Dr. Gellerman promising to write a letter of recommendation to the Navy and to put Northwestern's political clout to work for me. And he wanted me to see the Dean of the Music School, Dr. John Beatty.

I made an appointment to see Dean Beatty. When I laid out my plight before him, he got red in the face and incensed over the allegation of effeminates and homosexuals in the school. He angrily paced the office floor, shouting and waving his arms in contempt of the Navy recruiters, and rattling off names of sports figures and respected business men of influence who were lovers of music. Boy, was he mad!

The next day, Dean Beatty called the commandant of the Naval District in the Chicago area and gave him a piece of his musician's mind (in a manner not at all effeminate).

It wasn't long afterwards that the Navy recruiting office invited me down for a second interview, and I was ready for a fight. Lincoln Maythem, the ranking recruiter, opened the match by sparring around.

"We've had a couple of calls from Northwestern University. We don't know what this is all about, but we want to interview you again," he said, in the conciliatory tone of a peacemaker, while forcing his smile.

The other recruiters, lead by the basketball player, were more direct. They came after me like heavyweight bulldogs, and were obviously on the defensive as a result of having been called on the carpet by a superior officer. "What gives you the idea we rejected you for being an effeminate and temperamental musician?"

"I saw my file folder."

"It doesn't say any such thing!"

"The hell it doesn't!" I yelled, following Dr. Gellerman's advice to interject some four-letter words. (I'll have to admit, it made me feel good to respond so forcefully.)

"Now wait a minute," bristled one of the bulldogs, "Do you know who you're talking to?"

"I don't give a damn!" I snapped. "Open my file folder and see for yourself!" (My confidence was growing.)

"I don't think that'll be necessary," interceded Maythem. "But let's get down to brass tacks. Have you ever worked hard or done anything tough?"

"Have I ever! Let me ask *you* something: Did any of you ever push a wheelbarrow of concrete 300 yards down a ramp? Did you ever scrub three floors of a bank building at five in the morning? Well, I have—and more."

While some of these men were college athletes, they probably had never done any hard labor, and I was making them squirm a little.

Maythem the peacemaker resumed his line of questioning: "What would you do, Galvin, if anyone ever called you a fairy?"

"I'd bust his damned nose!" I flashed back, handling rough language like a truck driver and growing more confident all the time.

The two recruiters looked at each other, and I think they bit the sides of their mouths to keep from grinning.

They sent me out of the room, and I thought, *Oh, no, not another long wait.* But no more than five minutes later, Lincoln Maythem came out to inform me I had been accepted.

Let me tell you, I was one happy fella as I made my way back to the rooming house that day. And I think those big shot athlete-recruiters had some different thoughts on selecting men after going a few rounds with me. While later in the Navy I met some men who had been big-name athletes, most of us were average, everyday guys.

Actually, being muscle-bound could hinder a guy from becoming a good pilot. As in the case of a guy I'll call Frank—a big, muscular guy. During Primary Flight Training, the instructors said they practically had to beat him over the head to keep him from choking the stick and to relax. He kept thinking that flying was something that required a lot of muscle. Strange as it sounds, flying requires less physical effort than driving a car, but it takes more coordination and smoothness of action.

It was ironic, really: There I was, trying my best to get into the Navy, when a lot of guys would just as soon have stayed out of the military and were drafted.

*Salvation for a Doomed Zoomie*

I was out to prove myself to the world. I was growing more self-confident and self-reliant—which was good in some ways, but detrimental in that I thought about and relied on God less and less.

By now I had developed the habit of talking tough and down-right dirty. I guess it made me feel more manly.

Ever since Pearl Harbor—that "Day of Infamy," I had felt destined to be a Navy pilot. And I knew it would take a lot more than some near-sighted recruiters to stop me.

# 5

# Getting Off the Ground

The plan was to finish college, then report for preliminary flight training at Glenview Naval Air Station. But the escalation of the war changed all that. The fighting in the South Pacific was intensifying, and by the spring of 1942, because of a critical demand for Navy fighter pilots, I was called to active duty ahead of schedule—just before final exams. It posed no problem, though; since my grades were high, I was excused from finals and received my degree.

It had taken four years of hard work and scraping, but I made it. I was a college grad! I could hardly believe it!

*John, you're a pretty remarkable guy,* I smiled to myself. *Yessir! "John Remarkable," that's who you are.*

I said good-bye to friends and faculty at Northwestern, then boarded a train back home to Burlington, to spend a few days with my family before reporting for active duty.

My life had changed so much in four years that it was almost too much for Mom and Dad to accept. Their Johnny boy had earned his college degree and was on his way to become a Navy pilot. Dad was proud (as only the Irish can be proud), and Mom, responding to her motherly instinct, bravely tried to hide her apprehension.

It was great being home; Burlington seemed smaller now, and friendlier. Wherever I went I felt like the boy who went away and came back a man! It was a good feeling to be looked up to as grown and mature, as a college grad and a soon-to-be Navy pilot.

Soon my brief visit drew to a close and it was time to venture forth into the *real* world.

A few days later, on May 9, I stepped off the train at Glenview. Located about twenty-five miles northwest of Chicago, Glenview had been a quiet bedroom suburb before the war. But now, with the Naval Air Station so busily turning out pilots, the town was a beehive of activity, with men and women in sharp military uniforms coming and going. I hailed a taxi and went straight to the Naval Air Station to report in.

NAS Glenview would be my home for the next thirteen weeks, during which time I would be indoctrinated into Navy life and learn the rudiments of flying.

The air station was undergoing a huge construction program. Recently completed were new barracks, a recreation hall, and a movie theater. Some of the streets were paved, but most were gravel—muddy most of the time.

I went in as a seaman third class, which was the lowest form of life in the Navy (a fact, I soon learned, that the Navy instructors took devilish glee in reiterating to all newcomers).

After checking in with the officer of the day at the front gate, I was sent directly to the ship's store to be outfitted. I was handed a pair of high-laced black shoes and itchy khaki uniforms (with no insignia), a black tie, and a garrison ("fore-and-aft") cap.

From there, a group of us were double-timed to our living quarters. The place was nothing but a big, drab looking barracks, two stories high, with forty double bunks to each of its four wings. The head had a community shower on one side, while wash basins lined one wall and a row of bare toilets lined the other. Believe me, it had not been designed with privacy in mind. If the Navy was the best branch of the armed services, as Dad had insisted, then I wondered what the others were like!

The last vestments of individuality were shed when the Navy barbers gave us all crew-cuts. Later, as I looked at myself in a mirror, I could only shake my head in self-pity at the sight of my homeliness, accentuated by the unwelcome return of my painfully protruding ears.

Sleep did not come easily that first night. Aside from the recurring thoughts of my first day in the Navy and speculations about tomorrow, the barracks was filled with the bothersome cacophony of snores, grunts and men talking in their sleep. Trying to go to sleep in my strange new bed, and irritated by an itchy wool blanket, I tossed and turned on my thin-mattressed bunk, and finally drifted off.

Sometime during the night, I was startled from my sleep by a blood-curdling cry and the thud of a body hitting the deck. Someone turned on the lights, and several of us gathered around a guy who was sitting on the deck in a daze.

*God!* I thought, *Is this what these guys go through here?*

After the dazed man gathered his senses, he explained what happened. He had just arrived that day, as did the rest of us. He was dreaming that he parachuted out of a plane, but that the chute didn't open. That's when he fell out of the top bunk. It struck me as odd that the thought of so remote an experience as parachuting would bring about a nightmare. Pilots only parachuted in an emergency, anyway—and that always happened to the other guy, right? We had a good laugh over it, then sat up and talked a long while. It helped ease tensions for all of us.

Beginning at five the next morning, we were indoctrinated to a daily routine that would change little for the duration of our training at Glenview. Our instructors ran us or double-timed us everywhere—to class, to the mess hall, to the drill field, wherever. Because we ran through so much mud, our free time at the end of the day was spent hand laundering uniforms and spit-polishing shoes. Most of each day was spent in the classroom, going through ground school, with no flying to start with. Since we got so little sleep at night, it was really hard sometimes staying awake in class. Actually, some of the instructors were so prosaic and their subjects so dull, that even with a good night's sleep it would have been difficult.

The Navy seemed to operate alternately between two extreme priorities: "hurry up" and "wait." When we weren't running somewhere, we were standing in line. Usually one followed the other: we'd have to run to our destination, then wait. And let me tell you, standing in line in the boiling sun of that hot, humid Chicago climate, wearing heavy, itchy khakis, is no fun! Where were the efficiency experts?

We had no time off and were on the go constantly, seven days a week. Most of us were too tired to go over to the recreation hall, and the movies at the theater weren't all that good.

I do remember one of the films, though. It was Walt Disney's "Dumbo." You can imagine how hard-up for entertainment we Navy men were to go see a kids' film.

Well, "Dumbo" sticks out so well in my memory because at that time, I was quite thin and, with short hair, my large ears were overly prominent. During the movie, when Dumbo started flying around, flapping his big ears, one of the guys in the audience yelled out, "Hey! That looks like Galvin!" It brought a bigger laugh than anything in the movie. After that, my nickname was Dumbo, and it followed me all my life.

Ralph Rosen was a redhead who, since childhood, was stuck with the nickname "Red." Used to a monicker, he had a nickname for everyone, and always called me Dumbo—

*always*. So he was mostly responsible for the name's sticking with me. Even to this day, whenever I run into an old Navy buddy, I'm greeted with, "Hiya, Dumbo!" Maybe the sight of my ears helps them to remember.

Red and I went to flight training together, then on to Norfolk and aboard a couple of aircraft carriers in the South Pacific. An electronics genius, he became a career officer and retired from the Navy a captain.

It was about that time that one more obstacle sprang up. The Flight Selection Board reviewed my medical records, and a question surfaced over my ear problem. It was serious, and I was faced with getting grounded out of flight training. The matter might have escaped the board's attention, except that, ironically, the same doctor who gave me my induction examination was now at Glenview as a member of the Medical Board, and obviously had not forgotten his earlier encounter with me.

My hearing problem stemmed from the numerous ear infections I suffered as a small boy, which required having my eardrums lanced. The Navy doctor explained that scar tissue and calcium deposits had formed on my ear drums, which rendered them too rigid to quickly adjust to the sudden air pressure changes pilots experience in diving aircraft. The result could be dizziness, pain or even ruptured eardrums; any of which could jeopardize the safety of a pilot and his aircraft.

I couldn't believe it! Here we go again.

Well, I wasn't about to quit now. Round two was coming up. I went to discuss the matter with the flight surgeon. I gave him a convincing argument about my desire to become an aviator, and he rather apologetically said, "Well, if you want to get in that bad, I won't stop you."

It was a happy day when my class completed ground school and went out to the grassy field which was used for airplane takeoffs and landings. Waiting for us was a row of N3N "Yellow Peril" biplanes, one of which would give me my first experience in the air.

An Ensign instructor named R. A. Lewis took me up for my first flight. Those Yellow Perils had two open cockpits— for the instructor in front and his student pilot in back.

As I looked on from the rear seat, Ensign Lewis taxied the N3N clear of the row of parked planes, then stopped to rev up the engine in preparation for takeoff.

*This thing's gonna shake to pieces,* I thought, as the engine turned faster and faster. Then we started rolling across the sod and finally were airborne. I looked over the side at the ground falling away beneath us. What a sight!

Being in the air gave me the strangest sensation. I couldn't imagine an environment more foreign to a human being. Maybe it is defying gravity in a plane that gives some pilots the feeling of transcending the bounds of mortality and spawns a devil-may-care attitude that prompts them to play at being God. Whatever causes it, I eventually got a big dose of it.

In-flight communication was done the old-fashioned way— by shouting. The front cockpit had a rear-view mirror so the pilot could see his student at all times.

"How do you like it?" Lewis shouted back, above the engine's noise.

"Oh, just great!" I yelled back.

"How much flying have you done?"

I shrugged sheepishly and made a "zero" sign with my hand: "None."

He laughed.

"Why in the world did you sign up to be a Navy pilot when you don't even know if you like to fly?"

I didn't want to tell him that I was desperate for the money.

"Well, you'd better make sure that your seat belt is fastened, because we're gonna find out if you like to fly."

"It's fastened," I shouted to him, cinching my belt a little tighter and wondering what he was going to do.

At that instant, he whipped the trainer into a half snap roll so that we were flying upside down. I had no time to react.

## Salvation for a Doomed Zoomie

There I was, hanging by the seat belt with my arms dangling out of the cockpit. I looked straight down at the ground, some 2000 feet below. If anyone was watching, it must have been some sight, the trainer flying upside down with me, ludicrously suspended by the seat belt, and everything but my rear end dangling out, flapping in the airstream. I hardly looked like a Greek god.

I signed up for *this?*

I couldn't blame the recruiters, though: they told me becoming a Navy pilot would be tough. Maybe I should have listened to those guys.

The next training flights were much less eventful. After only ten hours of dual flying with an instructor, I got my chance to solo. By now, I had made many takeoffs and landings unassisted by the on-board instructor, but now, being alone in the plane really made a difference psychologically. This time I was Don Quixote instead of his credulous and amusing squire, Sancho Panza.

My solo flight went without a hitch and did much to build my ego. Afterwards, I telephoned my parents to tell them all about it. Long distance connections weren't the best then, so I had to yell over the phone in order to be heard.

Dad, being his usual skeptical self, asked, "What? *You* flew in an airplane *all alone?*"

"Dad, what do you think 'solo' means?"

"Well, I'm not sure."

"Look, Dad, it means that I took the plane up all by myself."

"Well, *you* don't know how to do *that*, John," he chided.

"Of course, I do!" I raised my voice, my temper beginning to flare. "At least they give me credit for it. That's what they've been teaching me to do up here."

I had been so excited about soloing, and Dad had to deflate me. It was a humbling experience—but not the last I'd ever have.

On the final day of preliminary flight training, several of us took three of our instructors out to Murphy's Tavern in Glenview to celebrate our graduation and indulge ourselves in a hearty steak dinner. In our group were Ensign Lewis, Ensign Makay and one other, whose name I cannot recall.

Let me remind you that back home and at college I didn't gamble, or smoke, or fool around with girls, or drink. But that night at Murphy's Tavern, I wasn't about to order a coke and have my buddies make fun of me. So I had my first beer. There I was, cussing and drinking beer right along with the rest of them. It sure felt great to be a *man!*

As the evening wore on, one of the guys in our class, Morton Deutch, got a little loud and show-offish, thanks to the many beers he had consumed, and decided to put on a show for us—and everyone else in the tavern. Pretending he was speaking into a microphone, he stood up and announced, "All right now, you instructors have had your inning, now we're going to have some fun." With that, he started to mimic them. It was hilarious roasting, and everyone rolled with laughter.

Before the evening was over, Ensign Lewis retold the story about taking me up for my first plane ride, and how I was hanging out of the cockpit, upside down. And, of course, by now, Ensign Lewis had captured the attention of all the tavern's patrons, who were hanging on his every word.

"If ever I saw a deathmask, that was it!" he howled with laughter, and everyone in the tavern joined in.

They all thought it was funnier than I did, but my two beers helped me to laugh along with them.

After three months of ground school and pre-flight training at the Navy's "elimination base" at NAS Glenview, we transferred to NAS Corpus Christi, Texas, for basic and advanced flight instruction.

There, we advanced to formation flying, aerobatics, and finally instrument flying—in the Vultee SNV monoplane trainer. This was a plane with greater horse power than the

N3N we were used to flying at Glenview. The larger engine created considerable vibration, which earned it the nickname, "Vultee vibrator."

We then went to Kingsville, Texas for fighter pilot training in a big, 450-horsepower SNJ trainer with .30-caliber machine guns mounted in the wings. We practiced formation flying, stunt flying and gunnery—my favorite phase of training. I always did well at gunnery and made good scores, though I don't know if I was good or just lucky.

I remember thinking to myself: *So this is what it's going to be like in combat*, as I fired away at the targets—either on the ground or towed in the air by another airplane.

We graduated as ensigns with Wings of Gold in January 1943, and were shipped off to Opalaka Naval Air Station, near Miami, for more advanced fighter training. There, we stepped up to a bigger plane again—to the 1200-horsepower Brewster Buffalo, a fighter which had been retired from service in the Pacific and replaced with newer, more advanced aircraft.

The Brewster Buffalo was a good plane, but a little tricky to fly. It was so short that it could almost fly sideways, and it took some real effort to keep it under control.

All of those old Buffaloes suffered from too many hours of hard flying. They should have been dispatched to the bone yard instead of reassigned to the training command. Their paint was faded and peeling, and their heavily scratched windshields appeared to be laced with cobwebs. The engines had seen better days too. Because the planes were so worn out, the instructors only half-jokingly renamed them the "Ensign Eliminators." The unsettling truth was that the engines often conked out, forcing the student pilot to bail out.

The instructors wanted to get rid of the old planes in the worst way—so much so that we were told if our plane ever so much as belched black smoke to fly it over the swamps and bail out so that it couldn't be retrieved.

I never had to ditch mine, though some of my classmates had to hit the silk. The thought of parachuting ran a chill up my spine, but those who had done it said there was nothing to it. I didn't want to find out. I remembered the guy in Glenview who fell out of his bunk.

# 6

# Stretching My Wings

**I** was assigned to Navy Fighting Squadron Eight (VF-8) and reported to NAS Norfolk, Virginia, for still more training—a rigorous, accelerated flight program.

All of us in the squadron were young—in our early twenties. We came from all parts of the country and from a variety of social, economic and ethnic backgrounds. Our squadron roster read like a football team's line-up, and gave a clue to the great mix of nationalities represented: Beauchamp, Wilson, Vanderhoof, Mendoza, O'Boyle, Longino, Delesdernier, Brownscombe, Van Derlinden, McGuire, Czerney, Lamoreaux, Brown, De Golia, Gmitro, Gustafson, Heinzen, Campbell, Boyles, Hoel and McCuskey.

To my surprise, our administrative officer turned out to be Lincoln Maythem, the sympathetic recruiter from Chicago who had tried to help me. He remembered me, of course. Sometime later, after we knew each other better, he was very apologetic over the rough treatment the other recruiters had given me.

I suspected that Lincoln was keeping an eye on me, just to be sure I could cut it as a pilot. After all that tough talk I gave him and the other recruiters, I knew I was going to have to prove myself. I over compensated by increasing my use of profanity, and I adopted a more pronounced swaggering gait.

During the early days of our squadron's training, living together and spending our free time together, all of us got to know and care about each other. We worked hard together, shared each other's joys and sorrows, and saw ourselves and those around us molded into disciplined and efficient fighter pilots. Together we shared the anticipation and uncertainty of going off to war. It nurtured in us a deep sense of comraderie and *espirit de corps*.

Nearly every guy who came to the squadron with an attitude of self-sufficiency and independence soon shed all notions of being a loner. Everyone was infected by a deep-seated pride in Fighting Squadron Eight. The dedication to country and the war effort was matched by personal commitment to each other and determination to establish VF-8 among the most outstanding fighter squadrons in the Navy.

But before we could hope to distinguish ourselves in combat, we had to master the tricky skill of aircraft carrier operations—taking off from and landing on the pitching deck of a flattop at sea.

The Navy had us practice first on a runway on dry land that was marked off to simulate the markings on a carrier deck. It looked easy enough. Our training plane was the old, reliable SNJ two-seater. It was a good trainer because it could take off and land at low speed, which gave a pilot more reaction time and made flying the plane less critical. SNJs were also cheap to manufacture and repair, which was important, considering damage caused as the result of the high degree of pilot error in a training program.

On my first simulated carrier landing, I flew my SNJ around in a nose-high attitude, bank-turned and made an approach for the "deck." I lined up with the landing signal officer who was standing on the left rear corner of the marked-off landing area. I watched him like a hawk, because he would signal to me with flags to indicate whether my approach was high, low, fast, slow, or right down the groove.

I came in low over the edge of the "deck" with full flaps to slow my speed, abruptly pulled back on the throttle and set the SNJ down nicely on the runway.

*What a piece of cake!*

By the end of six weeks, after hours and hours of practicing mock carrier operations, we were finally considered ready to try the real thing.

Our practice carrier was the *Charger*, a jeep aircraft carrier operating in Chesapeake Bay. The *Charger* was nothing more than an old liberty ship with a flight deck erected on top. Not the most glamorous thing, but it served its purpose.

They say you will always remember your first try at landing on a carrier—and I found that to be true. The dimensions of the *Charger's* flight deck were exactly the same as the ones we were used to practicing with on the ground. But now, peering out the SNJ's cockpit at that tiny carrier sitting all alone in the ocean, the flight deck looked as small as a postage stamp! As I banked around to come in for a landing, I noticed the flight deck was gently rolling. What had been a piece of cake on land was nerve-racking with a carrier on the ocean! Everything had to be done with split-second timing. One bad judgment, a simple miscalculation, and they'd have to scrape me off the fantail. The tension was mounting. My heart quickened and so did my breathing. I felt perspiration break out on my forehead and under my arms, but my mouth was as dry as a ball of cotton. Mother Nature seemed to have given me moisture where I'd like dryness, and dryness where I'd like some moisture!

A wave-off! Too high!

I pushed the trottle forward and eased back on the stick. The SNJ nosed skyward, while below, the flight deck whisked past in a blur. I had played my approach too cautiously. I guess in the back of my mind I was afraid of coming in too low and crashing into the fantail—an overreaction not uncommon to qualifying pilots.

As I circled up and around for another approach, I wondered if Lincoln was watching me. I hoped not. I entered the landing path and was determined to brave it and take that plane in low, like I was supposed to. Ahead of me loomed the ominous stern of the carrier—a solid wall of steel! In I glided—but too high again!

Wave-off!

*Dammit!*

Up and around for one more try. This time I *had* to do it!

To my relief, this time my approach was right on the money. I came in over the stern and set the SNJ down on the pitching deck at the exact right spot, snatching the arresting cable with my tail hook. I felt the braking action of the cable, then, according to procedure, stood on the brakes with all my weight. My knees were knocking together so violently that I was afraid my shuddering feet might slip off the brake pedals and my plane would go rolling off the deck and into the sea. I couldn't imagine a more terrifying experience than to ditch at sea. If man was out of his environment in the air, the ocean was even a more hostile environment! Whatever faint primal urge I had to be around water was adequately satisfied in the bathtub.

My feet held steady, though, and I was able to bring the SNJ to a halt. I just wanted to sit there and catch my breath, because, believe me, the adrenalin was really racing through my veins. At least I had peace of mind about my strong kidneys. But I had no time to unwind. The plane handlers pushed the SNJ back a few feet, unhooked the cable, and pushed me up to the fly-off spot. Then, for the first time, I flew off the carrier (which was a little easier on the nerves than landing). I circled the bird back around for another landing. I lined up, glided in right on the money, and this time the SNJ nestled down on the first attempt.

I satisfactorily completed all eight required take-offs and landings and was then considered qualified for carrier operations in an SNJ. After all of my class were qualified, we were transferred to the main station at Norfolk and to our new fighter squadron, VF-8.

Let me mention that the squadron was actually reforming. It previously had been a combat squadron operating off the carrier *Hornet* and had seen action at Midway. After that tour of duty, VF-8 returned to the States in August 1942, was decommissioned, and most of its personnel were reassigned.

Then came an exciting bit of good news: we were to receive a brand new fighter—the Navy's hottest plane yet. It was the Grumman F6F Hellcat. This was a tremendous thrill because it meant a jump all the way up to 2000 horse-power. We were one of the very first squadrons to get the Hellcat. What an ego trip! Just call me Pegasus!

The plane's switches and instruments were ideally located, making the cockpit a pilot's dream. And no wonder, our air group commander, Andrew McBirney Jackson, was a fighter specialist at the Navy's Bureau of Aeronautics when the F6F was designed by Grumman.

The plane had a three-blade prop with twelve-inch wide blades. Nine feet of engine stuck out in front of the cockpit, blocking everything up ahead from view and making it impossible to see straight ahead when taxiing. About all we could do was taxi in a zigzag pattern, veering to the left and looking to the right, then veering to the right and looking to the left. On a carrier flight deck, we relied on the directional signals of the deck crews. It took some getting used to, but I got the hang of it.

We were unexpectedly ordered to fly our new Hellcats to Naval Auxiliary Air Station, Pungo, Virginia, an isolated place

Fighting Squadron Eight was among the first to fly the Navy's new
F6F Hellcat.

nine miles from Virginia Beach. Then we discovered why: the
Navy wanted to keep its new fighter out of sight of the many
known and suspected spies who operated in the Norfolk area.

The big push was on to get fighter pilots trained, and we
were kept on the go seven days and three nights a week. After
a while it seemed as though our airplanes were a part of us,
and flying was becoming as natural a reflex as scratching an
itch. And that's the way the Navy wanted it.

The only unpleasant thing about training under such a
rigorous schedule was that we had very little time for liberty
in Virginia Beach. We got a half day off every other week,
from noon until 1800, which was hardly enough time for any
carousing (which I'd never done, but was intrigued to try).

Qualifying in the SNJ did not automatically qualify us for carrier operations in Hellcats, so we had to qualify all over again. This called for more practice mock carrier operations on land before we could operate off a carrier. Our training also included drills in formation night flying.

The Hellcat was considerably different from flying the much smaller and lighter SNJ. It was at least two and a half times its weight and had entirely different flight characteristics.

More good news arrived: our squadron would be attached to the new aircraft carrier, U.S.S. *Intrepid*, which was being outfitted at the naval shipyard. While waiting for the work to be completed so we could go aboard, we continued training in our Hellcats for almost five more months—a comparatively long time.

A few days before the *Intrepid's* commissioning, I received a letter from my parents, saying they were coming to Norfolk to see me.

*What for?* I wondered. They could hardly afford such an expensive trip, and neither of them had ever traveled more than fifty miles from home. I decided to phone home and find out.

Mom answered the call and I asked why they were coming. Over the phone I sensed her puffing up with pride as she told me they had received a *personal, engraved invitation* to the *Intrepid's* commissioning from the *admiral*!

Dad always wanted to see the ocean, and now was his chance. I reserved a room for him and Mom in a boarding house on the beach. After they arrived, Dad enjoyed sitting on the veranda, hours on end, watching the surf break and the tide come in. For a Midwesterner from Burlington, Iowa, Dad was particularly fascinated with the ocean.

The *Intrepid* was commissioned on August 16, 1943 at the Newport News Shipbuilding & Dry Dock Co., at Newport News, Virginia, with Capt. Thomas L. Sprague in command.

Commissioning day was a big affair, with thousands of people present. The Navy band was playing and the ship's company and our squadron were reviewed by the admiral, Captain Sprague and other members of the official inspection party, which included a number of high ranking Naval officers, politicians and various dignitaries.

I was wearing my khaki flight uniform, and I thought I looked rather dashing. It did something to my self-esteem that caused me to swagger a little more confidently. There was a mystique about fighter pilots then (and I suppose there still is), and my ego was rapidly getting caught up in it. Even Mom and Dad were impressed with me. Every once in a while, our eyes would meet, and when I saw the pride written all over their faces I felt great.

After the commissioning ceremony, civilian guests were invited aboard the *Intrepid*, and Dad got to explore every square foot—the flight deck, hangar deck and island (the superstructure sticking up off to the side of the flight deck). He looked over all the guns, inspected aircraft and was briefed on some new electronic survielance device called radar. He sure was impressed.

Our skipper, Lieutenant Commander William Collins, invited our parents out to Pungo to see our new Hellcats. They were permitted to go down by the planes and even climb aboard if they wanted.

I helped Dad up onto a wing so he could look in the cockpit. He was amazed at all the switches, gadgets and dials. He kept asking, "What's this? What's that?" And I told him what every switch and instrument was for.

"How come you know all these things?" he asked, frowning with confusion.

His provocation caused that old familiar tension to begin swelling up inside me, and I answered impatiently: "That's what they taught us in flight school!"

He climbed into the cockpit and wedged himself down into the seat. Being a plumber and accustomed to working with his hands so much, he was almost like a blind person who relied on touch to enjoy and appreciate things. He ran his fingers almost sensuously over the instrument panel, delicately touching every gauge, switch and button. But it was the joystick that captured his attention. As his hands lingered on it, I could sense the spawning of an instant love affair and knew he must have been thinking what a thrill it would be to fly that plane.

"What's this?" he asked, pointing to a button on the front of the joy stick.

"That's the gun trigger, Dad. It's all electrically controlled. I can fire all six machine guns, or I can cut out two and fire only four. See that chunk of glass right in front of your face? That's the gunsight. A lighted circle comes on, and when you get a target centered, you just squeeze the trigger."

As I explained things, Dad would either nod his head with understanding or slowly shake it in amazement.

"That button on top," I pointed out, "is called the pickle—the bomb release. We usually carry a 500 pounder."

Dad shifted his eyes up to me and asked with a skeptical squint: "How come you know all these things?"

*Here we go again!*

"I *fly* the airplane, Dad. I *have* to know."

But before the conversation got heated again, Commander Collins strolled over to my plane. He was telling all of us pilots that we were going to put on an air show for our guests (which was probably against regulations, but he thought they would appreciate it).

"C'mon, Dad, you've got to get out of the plane and go stand on the sidelines, because we're gonna put on a show for you."

"Where?"

"In the air!"

And then he had the audacity to ask me, "Well, who's gonna fly *your* airplane?"

I was so exasperated that I don't remember the expletive I chose to reply with. But I do remember the look of surprise on Dad's face, because he had never heard me talk that way at home. Before that day he had only heard me swear once, and that time he knocked me backwards out of a kitchen chair, and I went sprawling across the floor into the next room.

"Dad," I said, thumping a pointed finger against my chest and trying to be patient, "*I'm* gonna fly my *own* plane."

He said nothing, but threw me that old, familiar look of skepticism. Then he took Mom by the arm and slowly escorted her over to the spectators' area.

*Wasn't he ever going to let me grow up and give me credit for anything?* It really frosted me!

But it was soon forgotten, and minutes later I was in the air with the rest of the squadron, putting on a dazzling show for our parents. We did some formation flying and aerobatics, strafed some ground targets, and did some skip-bombing—coming in low and releasing the bomb. It was quite a buzz job, as we called it then.

Afterwards, I thought I detected a little pride behind the excitement in Dad's eyes. Mom was amazed beyond anything she had ever experienced, and all afternoon all she could say was, "For pity sakes! For pity sakes!"

That night, after a dinner party hosted by the skipper, Mom and Dad boarded a train back to Burlington. I was glad they came.

Three or four months later, after my squadron had gone on board the *Intrepid* and headed out to the war zone, I received a letter from Mom. She and Dad had gone to a movie at the Rialto Theater on Saturday night, and on the Pathe Newsreel saw the Navy's new "secret weapon" flash across the screen—the Hellcat! She wrote that Dad almost floated right out of his seat with pride because his own flesh and blood son flew one of those incredible new planes—and because *he* himself had sat in one! I could just visualize the whole thing, and it made me smile.

I put the letter aside and remembered back when my folks came out to Pungo and Dad sat so proudly in the cockpit of a Hellcat. The letter and the memories it stirred really warmed my heart.

# 7
# Narrow Scrape

The *Intrepid*, with a wartime crew of 3000 officers and enlisted men, was the newest of the *Essex* class aircraft carriers and held the distinction of being one of the largest warships in the American fleet.

Those of us in Air Group Eight were like tenants, not part of her permanent crew—or ship's company, as they are called. Since the crew was new aboard the ship and had yet to establish its turf, we were spared the usual "us" and "them" separatism or outright rivalry found on veteran carriers.

The *Intrepid* was totally self-contained, truly a floating city. It was the last word in efficiency, technological advancements and functional design. Everyone had an assigned place for work, combat, meals, sleeping, rest and relaxation.

At our disposal was the day's most modern on-board communications system, with an intricate telephone network and public address system.

Large as the *Intrepid* was, she was easy to get around on. At the most, a five-minute walk would get you any place on board you wanted to go. It was that compact and that well laid out.

Let me backtrack to explain the composition of an air group. Ours had a fighter squadron, dive bomber squadron and torpedo squadron. We were aviators only, on board solely to use the carrier as an ocean-going airbase. The running of the ship was left to its crew.

Air Group Eight gave the *Intrepid* a full complement of planes. In VF-8, we had fifty-five fighter pilots and thirty-six F6F Hellcats. The dive-bomber squadron, VB-8, had forty-two pilots plus crew, and twenty-four Curtiss SB2C Helldivers. Torpedo squadron VT-8 had twenty-four pilots, plus crew, and eighteen TBM Avenger torpedo bombers.

I should mention also that the torpedo bomber carried a crew of three, including the pilot, while a dive bomber was a two-man plane. Our Hellcats, of course, were single seaters.

Right after Air Group Eight boarded the *Intrepid*, the ship left port for a two-week shakedown cruise. Sailing down into the Caribbean, the ship and all its equipment and systems were operated at full speed and maximum usage. This created extreme vibration—literally a shake-down—to spot problems that would have to be remedied before heading into a war zone.

For most of us on board, it was our first experience at sea. Back in Iowa, I'd been around some large lakes and wide rivers, but being afloat on the ocean placed me in the middle of a watery world beyond anything I'd ever experienced.

The sea, I soon learned from the old salts, had many moods. Maybe that's why they called her "she." And in many ways the ocean does have some womanly characteristics. At times, she can be romantically calm and peaceful—almost placid, her smooth surface broken only by friendly, playful dolphins that delight in making those repetitive arching lunges out of the water described as dolphining. Then the sea can be a lively mistress, caressed by a breeze, challenging, adventurous and beckoning. Swells sensuously undulate as schools of flying fish dart from crest to crest. It is times such as these that sailors lose their heart to her. And then there are times she can be whipped by a storm into a she-devil kind of fury, with waves up to ninety feet that can capsize smaller sailing craft. And, like a woman's influence on a man, the sea's changing moods can affect a sailor's emotions. But these were things that I had heard and, for the most part, had not experienced, for I was just as uninitiated about women as I was about the sea.

With the shakedown repairs completed and with Air Group Eight aboard, the *Intrepid* departed Norfolk on December 3, 1943. After we were at sea, the word went out that our destination was San Francisco, by way of the Panama Canal. That was good news to us, because San Francisco had the reputation of being a good liberty town.

Our squadron adapted quickly to carrier life, and you couldn't have found a more motivated bunch of pilots. We were flying the Navy's newest fighter and operating off the largest, most modern aircraft carrier in the world. How could we not have inflated egos?

Our squadron commanding officer, Commander Collins, was called "The Skipper," "The Old Man" and various other names, many of which wouldn't be appropriate to mention here. He was a gung-ho graduate of the Naval Academy, where I am convinced some of the students major in pettiness. True to Navy blue, he did almost everything by the book.

The Skipper was also crazy about organ music. This led to Eddy Osborn joining our squadron. Eddy was an instructor at one of our training bases, and when the skipper found out he was an organist, he brought him on board. Now, Eddy wasn't an ordinary, run-of-the-mill organ player; he was really gifted. It seems that before the war he was a professional organist in one of Chicago's large theaters.

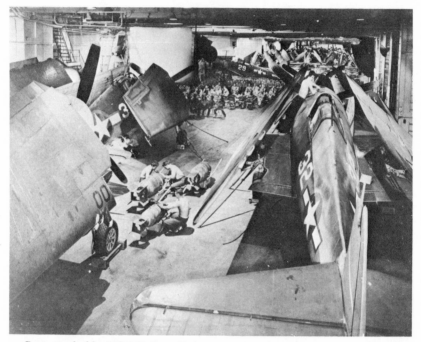

Surrounded by F6F Hellcat fighters, ordnancemen work on bombs on the hangar deck of a carrier. Officers and men in the background watch a movie. The *Intrepid* also had organ concerts.

To show you how far gone Collins was on organ music, he scrounged around and got a Hammond organ donated to the squadron. Somehow he convinced some sentimental, patriotic soul that organ music was just what sailors wanted to hear in their off-duty time.

Then Collins pulled some rank and got a stage erected on a bulkhead of the hangar deck, so Eddie, at the organ, could entertain the crew. At nighttime the area was transformed into a miniature concert hall, and sometimes Eddie would attract a fair-size audience. Naturally, because of my love for music, I was right there almost every night, enjoying the concert. Eddie was a nice guy, and he contributed much to the entertainment of all hands.

But back to Collins' penchant for going by the book. Everything was by the numbers. Sometimes that's okay, but other times it can be a real pain in the neck. When we checked in aboard the *Intrepid*, for instance, the skipper decided to personally assign us our quarters. He came up with this ridiculous idea of assigning us roommates by pairing us off by the sequence of our Navy serial numbers. My number was 250594, and for a roommate, I was given the pilot with the next serial number in sequence. We had absolutely no choice in the matter. None of us could imagine a worse way of doing it. But that's the way it was with the skipper, no leeway at all. With him, it was rigid military procedure all the way.

Now, I don't want to make it appear that we didn't like Collins, because we did. When it came down to military savvy, we respected—even admired—him. He was a highly intelligent man and an outstanding flyer. We all had to agree that no one could give us the valuable kind of training that he did. Drill, drill, *drill*—all the time. It was repititious and tiresome, but after a while, we began to see that we were getting *good*! Most of the men in the squadron are still alive, thanks to the training they received from Collins.

Training was always serious business, but one day Collins and big, old Gus had a humorous confrontation. Collins was always saying, you automatically do this, and you automatically do that. Let me tell you, after we'd heard that for the umpteenth time, we were fed up with it! One day, Gus made a landing pass at the carrier without putting down his hook, and later, when he did get down and we were having our debriefing in the ready room, Collins really castigated him, berating him in front of all the rest of us pilots, yelling that "There's no excuse for forgetting to lower your landing hook! It's something you just *automatically* do!"

Well, old Gus wasn't one to be pushed around by anyone, and he blurted out: "Well, dammit, skipper, I've never been able to find that automatic button on my plane!" We all roared with laughter, and that just made Collins furious!

Once the *Intrepid* had put out to sea, we got as much time in the air as possible, usually practicing attacks against a target sled towed 1000 yards behind the carrier. We'd take off as if we were going after a real enemy target, the fighter pilots escorting the dive bombers and torpedo bombers at 25,000 feet.

Some of the fighters started the attack by diving down for a strafing run. Next came a wave of dive bombers with some fighter escorts right beside them. Last, coming in at a low angle of attack, were the torpedo bombers with some fighter escorts. Sometimes, to conserve ammunition, the attacks were simulated—minus bombs and bullets. We always grumbled about it because it wasn't a lot different from kids pointing their fingers at the "bad guys" and shouting, "Bang! Bang!" We called these practice attacks "group gropes," and they generally took about four hours to complete.

In addition to giving us gunnery practice, the group hops also helped to improve our carrier landings and takeoffs. Sometimes we were catapulted, and other times we flew off without assistance. We usually repeated this routine a couple of times a day.

All of us had our turns at combat air patrol. This is the carrier's protective patrol, and it worked this way: four or eight fighters were stacked at 5000-foot intervals in the vicinity of the carrier, keeping their eyes open for the enemy. It was really boring, unchallenging work. All I did was sit up there, high over the carrier, making left-hand turns all day. If the radar saw enemy planes, then the fighter director officer would order us to intercept. We practiced this monotonous procedure constantly, hour after hour. By the end of a flight, I was hot and sweaty and not very good company.

It was more fun for the boys in the radar room. They pretended that we were enemy planes and got some helpful drills out of it.

The most hair-raising thing about carrier operations is landing at night. This is very hazardous, terrifying work, and some pilots never get over the anxiety of doing it. Come to think of it, I don't know very many pilots who said they ever got used to it. I never did!

Flying around out there in the darkness, preparing to land on a carrier, we were like a bunch of bats, winging back to the black sanctuary of their cave. Real bats, however, with their built-in sensory devices, had the advantage, because in those days we had to return to the carrier without airborne radar.

Landing on a carrier at night was done this way: you make the usual approach to the carrier, except that you line up on a completely blacked-out carrier—almost flying blind. Inside the cockpit, the only light comes from the instrument panel and its reflection off the windows of the cockpit. Everything outside is a black void. Far below, the carrier is marked only by a double row of tiny, jewel-like lamps that sparkle faintly. These lights are recessed into the flight deck so not to be seen by prowling Jap submarines. Pilots can't see them either— until the last fifteen degrees of a turn, fifty feet off the water and only 300 yards from the carrier. Those are the only lights: no flood lights, no landing lights—nothing but those tiny little lamps on either side of the landing area.

What a tense moment, coming in for a night landing! It takes total concentration and coordination. You can see those little lights for only seconds before setting down. Your temples are pounding and you're sweating blood, straining your eyes to see something other than just those lights. Then you touch down, and your wheels skid and screech on making contact with the deck. You hold your breath and brace in anticipation for the tail hook to catch on the arresting cable. If you're not lined up properly for the landing and have to take a wave-off, then you circle around and try it again. And that just adds to the tension—especially when your fuel is running low, and you know that if you don't get down soon, you'll have to ditch at sea.

## Salvation for a Doomed Zoomie

Carrier landings were always tense.

As soon as your plane touches down on the flight deck, you know in an instant when you catch the cable, because it jerks the plane to a halt in only a few yards. What a relief.

Landings were always precarious, but take-offs had their potential hazards too. The thing we feared most about takeoffs—whether during the day or at night—was to lose power and hit the drink in front of the ship and maybe get sliced in half by the knife-like bow. That's why, right after taking off, we always veered to the right (regardless of the admiral's insistance that we follow the book and take off straight ahead).

If a pilot had to ditch at sea, he was picked up by a destroyer (helicopter pick-ups came in another time and another war). A Hellcat would usually float for two or three minutes—not

92

a lot of time, but usually enough for the pilot to climb out of the cockpit.

Collins insisted that all of us stay in top physical shape, and he ran a very good athletic program that included my favorite sport—touch football.

Once when I was playing on the line, a little fellow across from me was giving me a bad time. The center snapped the ball and I charged this little guy. But he jostled me back about ten feet and set me down hard on my rear-end. Well, I got up and just couldn't believe this guy could push me around that way. We ran the next play. The ball was snapped and once more the guy elbowed me back out of the play.

"Who is that squirt?" I asked Gus.

"Don't you know, Dumbo? He's Rudy Gmitro."

I recognized the name right away. Rudy was the star halfback for Minnesota when they were in their prime. He was only about five-ten and 160 pounds, but he was just like a steel spring, pushing me back the way he did.

We also had Jim Hodak in our squadron. He was an outstanding football player and wrestler from Michigan. Then there was Bob Hobbs, an all-conference basketball player from the University of Iowa, and Don Carney, who made little All-American as a halfback from Ripon College in Kansas, as well as Bill Lamoreaux, who made crew for the University of California varsity rowing team. And back in the States, one of the station officers was the famous Killer Kane. What power houses! You talk about touch football being *rough*. We had some talented athletes.

I really liked getting to know those guys, and I guess one thing that helped me to enjoy carrier duty a little better was the fraternity sort of life we had—something I had missed in college because of my busy schedule with part-time jobs.

While most of us pilots in VF-8 were green and right out of flight training, there were two or three who had seen combat. Of those, Scott McCuskey from Arkansas, was the most seasoned. He had already shot down six Jap planes and received the Navy Cross. All of us looked up to Scott because of his knowledge of what war was really like.

Boydstun, Heinzen and Hobbs came to us from a previous tour of carrier duty, as did Whitey Feightner, who was the second most savy combat pilot we received. Collins and Ron Hoel, our executive officer, had no previous combat experience.

Not surprisingly, the skipper only taught us what the academy taught—mostly theory. So after he'd leave the room, or later, after we returned to our quarters, everyone would congregate around McCuskey while he told us what the war was *really* like and how to fly and fight to win and live—all definitely not according to the book.

"You do what the skipper tells you in combat and you'll be dead," Scott used to warn us. Let me clarify that he wasn't purposefully being insubordinate and had nothing personal against the skipper; he wanted to help us stay alive. He had a stabilizing effect on our squadron, and many of us returned from the war alive because of what we learned from him.

More than anything else, Scott emphasized the importance of teamwork. To him it was the cardinal rule for survival— and believe me, it was drilled into our heads over and over.

"Stay with the group," Scott tried to impress upon us, "don't try to be a hero by taking on the enemy alone."

We heard that so often it began to sound like a broken record. Yet how quickly we can forget.

The *Intrepid* arrived at the entrance to the Panama Canal and slowly began the transit through the narrow locks and canals that would take us from the Atlantic Ocean to the Pacific Ocean.

Even to a lifelong land-lubber like me, the locks seemed very narrow—certainly not built for ships as large as the *In-*

*trepid.* The ship displaced 27,100 tons, was 872 feet long, had a beam of ninety-six feet, and a draft of almost twenty-eight feet. That's a lot of ship! And the going had to be careful in order to make it through without damaging either the ship or the sides of the locks and canals.

We made it through the first set of locks, then sailed across the lake and into the canal leading to the second set of locks. On the flight deck strutted the canal pilot, wearing his big panama hat and smoking a long, black Havana cigar. Some of the guys resented his freedom to smoke, because for us the smoking lamp was always out on deck.

A bridge had been errected across the flight deck, from port to starboard, so the pilot could see the sides of the ship. All he did was walk back and forth—an easy job we grumbled.

Near the city of Balboa, while negotiating an S-curve too slowly, the *Intrepid* drifted dangerously too close to one side of the canal. This caused the suction from the screws to pull the stern to port which turned the bow starboard. As hundreds of us watched helplessly, the bow rammed the side of the canal three times, causing serious damage to the carrier and the side of the canal.

The pilot frantically ran back and forth, and everyone was shouting. It was mass confusion. The captain was red-faced with anger. It was a little humorous at first, but then we heard the damage reports and realized how serious it was.

The bow had been ripped open below the water line, and the carrier was taking on water. The flooded compartments were sealed off by locking their water-tight doors, and that kept the ship from taking on more water and possibly sinking. That, of course, would have closed the canal and caused our war ships to sail the long, treacherous route around the horn of South America.

But there was another problem—trying to navigate northward through rough seas to a deep-water port at Alameda Naval Yards in San Francisco Bay. The engineers decided the best remedy was to patch the hull with concrete. It would take a few days to accomplish the tricky task, and this idle time gave us an opportunity for some much welcomed time ashore.

Although the city of Balboa wasn't the safest place for an American sailor, and the people weren't all that friendly, this was a chance to get away from shipboard routine.

True to the image of seagoing men, many of the guys traded juicy stories about their prowess with women. But most of it was just that—talk—a lot of hot air. In reality they were just as naive and inexperienced as I was. Several of the guys did go ashore, and one night some buddies gleefully told me they had met a beautiful girl from my hometown who remembered me from high school and wanted to see me. They told me her name, and I recognized it immediately. I remembered her as a gorgeous, voluptuous girl.

Well, believe me, I wasted no time in trying to contact her. But I never succeeded. And just as well, because I learned later that she was a madam at a local brothel.

After five days, temporary repairs to the *Intrepid* were complete. It took 250,000 barrels of concrete to seal the bow, and now the ship was ready to limp on to Alameda.

Right after we passed through the canal an amazing thing happened. It concerned my Mom. Now she was a small-town gal and had never been anywhere in her life. She was effervescent and loved being around people, but was a little absent minded and often got names confused. On top of that, she was a bit eccentric about a lot of things.

In one of her letters she wrote: "Bob Amsberry [my boyhood chum who lived across the street] is in the Navy, his mother told me. You be sure to look for him out there."

Can you believe that? I had to shake my head and laugh. *For Pete's sake, Mom,* I thought, *Don't you know how big and spread out all over the world the Navy is?*

A few hours later, right after we emerged from the canal that passed through the city of Balboa and were heading out into the Pacific Ocean, an announcement came over the loudspeaker: "Ensign John Galvin, report to the signal bridge."

I couldn't imagine why anyone would want me up on the signal bridge, but I headed that way in a rush, wondering what I had done wrong now.

The signal bridge is located near the captain's quarters and is part of the island. It is several decks high and houses, among other facilities, the signal bridge, which is the equivalent of an airport control tower. It also is the communications center of the carrier.

I arrived at the signal bridge and told the signalman on duty why I was there.

"Here, this is for you," he said, handing me a teletype message. It was from a picket boat, sailing somewhere near the entrance to the Canal Zone. It read: "Good luck, and good hunting," and it was signed, "Bob Amsberry"! Through his job as a signalman, he apparently knew that the carrier departing Balboa was the *Intrepid*, and through his Mother knew I was aboard.

Didn't I tell you my Mom was amazing?

The *Intrepid* sailed further westward, into the open waters of the beautiful blue Pacific. She was a stately ship, but because of the tremendous weight of the concrete in her bow, she rode in the water with a three- to four- degree down angle. It was a little pathetic.

Word was received that there wasn't an available drydock anywhere on the west coast, and we would berth at Alameda to wait our turn for repairs. It was discouraging, because we were itching to get to the war zone. How long we would be delayed was anyone's guess.

# 8
# Journey Into War

We sat around the bachelor officers quarters at Alameda for two months, not knowing when the *Intrepid* would be repaired. It was frustrating: we were desperately needed to help fight the war in the Pacific, but there we were, stuck at Alameda. It made waiting all the tougher.

Commander Collins kept us on a rigorous training schedule and, in off-duty hours, we had liberty in Oakland, and hung around the Navy recreational facilities.

On Sundays, for lack of other things to do, I attended chapel services—and that's almost the only time of the week I ever thought about God. Like a lot of the guys, I carried a New Testament in my luggage, only I never read it.

Christmas arrived, and I dreaded the lonesome feeling I would have being away from family and friends. But I was happily spared the agony when one of our pilots, Dick DiGolia, whose wealthy grandfather owned the St. Francis Hotel in San Francisco, took me to spend the day with his family at their luxurious Palo Alto home.

I'd never been around people that well-to-do, so it was quite an eye-opener for a poor boy from Burlington, Iowa! Instead of their being aloof, as I thought all rich people were, they were very friendly and hospitable. They made my Christmas much more enjoyable than the previous one at Corpus Christi, which was lonely and depressing. So I must admit that I was mostly caught up in the festive traditions of Christmas and never seriously looked at it as the celebration of the birth of the Savior, Jesus Christ.

While waiting weeks for the *Intrepid* to be repaired, our squadron began survival training. It was a fun diversion—except for the swimming test.

Since I wasn't a good swimmer, and hated being in the water as much as a cat does, the whole water survival training was unpleasant. The worst part came when I had to jump into the swimming pool fully dressed and swim around in a circle for twenty minutes. The first minute in the water wasn't so difficult, but then it became a real struggle trying to stay afloat. As if I didn't have enough trouble, some of the guys standing on the pool deck were getting a good laugh from watching me. Humiliation was one thing I didn't need right then.

*Why do I have to do this?* I asked myself. I really didn't see much purpose in it—particulary since we pilots always flew with life jackets and inflatable rubber rafts. Who worried about getting shot down over water, anyhow? The odds were one in a million it would happen to me! I'd just take my chances.

But there I was, floundering through a boring, tiresome, humiliating swimming test. The longer I flailed around in the water, the more upset I became. I don't get angry often, but right in the middle of that swimming test, I finally got so fed up from choking and swallowing water that I thought, *Nuts with this!* Gasping and sputtering water, I paddled to the side of the pool and climbed out.

I was fully clothed and sloshing wet and must have looked like a half-drowned rat. (I was as mad as one!) In front of the whole class, I walked up to the instructor and told him right to his face: "That's all for me!"

He was a little startled and didn't take it too kindly. Not surprisingly, I flunked the test. Luckily, the bad mark didn't stop me from flying, but it was a blemish on my record which would weigh against me.

Long-awaited orders finally came through for our squadron to move out—to sail for Pearl Harbor. At last! We were going to the war zone!

To our surprise, we were going to sail on the *Intrepid*. Although the carrier was still awaiting repairs, she was seaworthy, and the Navy decided to put her to use as a transport— for our air group plus several thousand additional troops. Boy, was it crowded on board.

Because of the ship's severe down-angle caused by the concrete in her bow, we couldn't conduct flight operations off her deck. For all practical purposes, she was just a barge. And that's what we called her—the "Royal Barge." But the stigma didn't stick for long.

Months later, after I had left the *Intrepid* and she received her repairs, she finally made her debut in the war zone, and went on to distinguish herself in many combat operations. She survived the war a gallant ship, and went on to serve her country with valor in Korea and Viet Nam. Though my tour of duty aboard the *Intrepid* was short and uneventful, I was proud to have been aboard.

We were unloaded on the island of Maui, and set up housekeeping at Puunene Field, which had a 3200-foot runway. Puunene is a native name that means *Goose on the Mountain*. I've heard some odd Indian names for cities and rivers back in Iowa, but I never heard of anyone naming a place *Goose on the Mountain*. Can you imagine living in a town called *Goose on the Mountain*, Iowa?

Puunene was our home for the next five months, while we waited for assignment to another carrier. Since we weren't in the war zone, there wasn't much to write home about except our training and the beautiful places we visited on the island. I wrote often to Mom and Dad—and to Claire Hill, a pretty girl whom I had met and dated at Northwestern.

There were some things we were not allowed to write about in our personal letters—information on troop movements and so forth. And you can understand why: people back home might innocently talk about such news and it could possibly fall into the hands of Jap spies who could use it to their advantage.

So, for security reasons, all outgoing mail was censored. The usual method was for restricted info such as dates, locations and other Navy matters to be blacked out with ink or cut out.

Censoring all that mail was a big job. Enlisted men's letters were censored by officers, and officers were supposed to censor other officers' letters. I emphasize "supposed to," because, in practice, we usually just signed off another officer's letter without looking at it, knowing everyone took security seriously.

On our arrival at Puunene, the skipper, true to his style, immediately started one of his ambitious training programs. We were training continuously—probably receiving three times the normal training of most squadrons.

Train, train, *train!* We must have been the best-trained outfit in the Navy. I didn't mind it, though, except for the swimming tests. The result of all this training was that we became a very close-knit group, and our performance showed it.

Gus, T.I., Chris and myself: the four of us became close friends, and because we worked well together we became an efficient flying team.

Gus always reminded us to stick together—in everything, whether on shore leave or in combat. It was the number one basic survival tactic, and it was drilled and drilled into our heads. No matter how tempting a target might be, we were never to leave our wingman and go after it alone. It could be a trap, with a flock of Zeros in the clouds, waiting like vultures to take off after a stray American fighter and shoot it down. Or it could be something else, equally disastrous.

On Maui, we got in a lot of trap and skeet shooting—not for pleasure, but for gunnery training. Firing at those moving targets was supposed to help us learn to "lead" a speeding Jap Zero. Fighter pilots, like the Marine's top ace, Joe Foss, who grew up with a rifle in his hands, had developed that skill in their youth, and it helped them score more hits against the enemy's planes.

It was during this phase of our training that I had my most shocking experience in the Navy—learning hand-to-hand combat. We were taught by the biggest, meanest Marines the Navy could find (back then, I thought *all* Marines were like that!). Volunteers for hand-to-hand combat demonstrations usually ended up half killed. It's not a gentleman's sport, and everything I ever learned about fair play, I quickly realized, had no place in hand-to-hand combat.

Imagine yourself unarmed and attacked by a killer-mad Jap with a knife or gun who wanted nothing more than to send you to your honorable ancestors. What do you do? How do you protect yourself and disarm the assailant? At first, such a situation seemed impossible, but the Marines taught us what to do. It wasn't very pretty, or gentlemanly, or honorable in any way, but it was designed to keep us from getting killed. And anyone who didn't like the methods being taught...well, the Marines had a name for guys who fought fair: *corpse!*

Survival training also focused on how to deal with the natural elements. When we climbed into the cockpit of a Hellcat, we were ready for whatever might happen, whether it was getting shot down over water or over dense, hostile jungle. Ditching at sea didn't sound too bad, because you could figure on quickly getting picked up by a float-plane or a submarine on lifeguard duty. But trying to survive in a Jap-overrun tropical jungle was something else.

Survival in the jungle depended to a large degree on how well you managed to live off the land. So we were taught which plants were edible and which ones were poisonous.

"The coconut," said an instructor, "is a downed pilot's best friend. If thirsty, drink the milk of an *unripe* coconut. But don't drink the milk of a *ripe* one—it will give you diarrhea." More than an inconvenience, diarrhea could lead to dehydration, loss of strength, and even death.

The Marines proved what they said about ripe coconuts causing diarrhea—by having us drink some! The effect was quick and convincing, and we all became instant believers. The meat of a ripe coconut is edible, though, and we were shown how to use a sharply pointed stick to open them.

Most of us resented the tougher-than-thou arrogance of those "Jarhead" Marines and never seriously thought we'd ever personally have to resort to using all that over-blown Boy Scout stuff. That shows how naive and ungrateful we were. But in time our attitude changed, mostly as a result of two pilots who had to bail-out over a jungle or crash-land in one. They had made it back only because they remembered what those Marines taught them.

We kept training while waiting for the *Intrepid* to be repaired, but there was delay after delay in getting the ship into a drydock. Meanwhile, our squadron was desperately needed in the south Pacific. So, at long last, we received orders to board another carrier, the U.S.S. *Bunker Hill* (CV-17), under the command of Capt. T. P. Jeter, which was the same size, class and design as the *Intrepid*, only a year older. We flew aboard during the first week of January 1944, and it was a day to remember—not only because of the excitement of going on board a veteran combat ship, but also because one of Mom's letters brought another laugh.

The U.S.S. *Bunker Hill*.

She had written a few days earlier that Ray Andrews' mother wanted me to be sure and look up her son who was somewhere in the Southwest Pacific on a carrier. Ray was a guy I had grown up with and went to Sunday School with every week at the First Methodist Church. Well, after the incident at Panama, I had to chuckle again at Mom's naivete. You just had to expect something like that from a small-town gal who didn't understand what the odds were against ever running across Ray in so vast an area. I pretty much dismissed the whole thing from my mind.

I landed my Hellcat on the *Bunker Hill*, and no more than parked it, when up walks a guy and yells out, "Hi, John." And I could hardly believe it! There he was, Ray Andrews!

Mom was unpredictable as they come, but she sure had an uncanny knack of foreseeing things like this happening.

*Salvation for a Doomed Zoomie*

I met one more familiar face on the *Bunker Hill*. He was Tom, the basketball player, one of the Chicago recruiters. He was a member of the carrier's flight deck crew and had a tough physical job, pushing planes around on the deck. I couldn't resist every opportunity to give him a good-natured jab by telling him how tough it was to be a fighter pilot and how soft it was to be a member of the flight deck crew!

The giant carrier was taking on fuel, ammunition and supplies in preparation to return to the war zone. The crew of 2700 was combat-tested—real veterans compared to those of us in the air group who, for the most part, were fresh, eager, young, and had never tasted combat.

We were the new tenants, but unlike the warm reception from the *Intrepid's* crew, the men on the *Bunker Hill* were cool and aloof. They let us know that Air Group Seventeen, which we replaced, had distinguished itself for courage and valor. It was a hard act to follow, as the men of the *Bunker Hill* kept reminding us.

It wasn't until the *Bunker Hill* left Pearl Harbor and was heading south on the open sea, that we were told our destination: the Marshall Islands.

Several times daily we practiced escorting, dive bombing and strafing. At day's end we were stiff, sweaty and smelly, and fatigued from sitting for hours in the cockpits of our planes, breathing pure oxygen.

The *Bunker Hill's* crew—officers and enlisted men—had been recently inducted into the Shellback Society for having sailed across the equator. Old salts take this Navy tradition very seriously. It dates back to ancient mariners who sailed the seas long before America had a Navy. The initiation was much like fraternity hazing in college. It has become subdued in the years since the war, but when I was made a shellback the process included crawling through a long canvas tunnel filled with garbage, running a gauntlet of shellbacks who beat us with lengths of rubber fire hoses, and kissing the "Royal Baby's" belly button (the Royal Baby being the fattest chief on board). The Royal Barber snatched handfuls of my hair and cropped it unevenly short. I had black and blue bruises for weeks, and that, coupled with my ridiculous haircut, made me look like one of today's punk rockers.

There were survival lectures every hour we weren't flying. Up till then, survival was something we took lightly. But on the *Bunker Hill* it was regarded much more seriously. This was because the ship had seen so many of her pilots ditch at sea or bail out over remote jungles. A number of those flyers never came back.

When it came to survival, we were the best-trained and best-equipped of all the world's pilots. We went through extensive training on how to use our parachute and other survival equipment, how to survive at sea and how to live off the land. Intelligence briefings familiarized us with the islands, the jungle and the kind of people we might encounter ("don't expect leis and kisses").

Preparing for flight started with the bare essentials. I stripped down to my Navy issue skivvies (which were like a low grade white gunny sack), put on my flight suit and then the zoot suit. That wasn't its official name, of course. It was more properly called an anti-blackout suit, anti-gravity suit, G-suit or pressure suit. A cross between a fat woman's corset and a dancer's leotards, it was as snug as a second layer of skin and fastened with all kinds of confusing laces and zippers.

This ingenious device would keep me from blacking out when pulling out of a steep dive at high speed. It had about fifty rubber bladders that were inflated with air and kept pressure against the torso and limbs. Without the suit, because of the force of gravity, blood would pool in my legs, and my heart wouldn't be able to pump enough blood to my brain. When the brain doesn't get enough blood, whammo! Blackout. With an unconscious pilot at the controls, a plane has only one way to go, and that's down.

After squirming into the zoot suit, next came the inflatable Mae West life jacket. It was called a Mae West because when

inflated it looked like...well, let's just say that if it were being named today, we'd probably call it a *Dolly Parton*.

A long, heavy machete was strapped to one leg, and a trench
knife or "frog sticker" strapped to the other one. My roots
were the heavy, high-laced field boots like the Marines wore.
Over all this came the detachable parachute harness.

"The tighter the straps the better," said the instructor. So
good old Galvin had his parachute harness cinched so tight
he couldn't stand up straight. Now, with plotting board in
hand, I was ready to fly.

Wow! Look out Japs, here comes God's gift to the war effort, decked out like an overstuffed moving van.

Fortunately, I didn't have to waddle across the flight deck
and climb into the plane wearing the forty pound parachute
pack (which also included an inflatable rubber raft and
emergency provisions). This was permanently stowed in the
seat of the plane.

One of the first things I did after climbing into the cockpit
was to attach my harness to the parachute pack, which doubled
as seat padding. The seat was a thin pad on the deflated raft
and emergency packet of survival equipment and supplies.

The emergency packet included such supplies as a weather
proof flashlight, die marker packs, signal mirror, concentrated
food tablets, matches, water purification tablets and a pon-
cho. The word was that the die marker was also effective in
keeping sharks away, so most of us carried a few extra packets.

Oh, yes, there was also a survival manual in the packet. I
think it was written by the same guy who writes assembly directions for kids' swing sets. If you like morbid literature, pick
one up at a Navy surplus store. Peace of mind it didn't bring,
and I was confident with it only so long as I never had to leave
the cockpit.

As I said, I never expected to be shot down, and neither
did any of the other guys—it always happened to someone
else. But just in case, I took some advice and removed the

foam padding from the seat cushion and put in cans of water and emergency food concentrates. Less cushion, more weight, but better chance for survival—unless you landed in water and weren't a good swimmer, then you'd sink like a rock.

In previous training, there was little instruction on parachuting, the rationale being that it was only for that rare emergency none of us was likely to have. But on the *Bunker Hill*, the attitude wasn't "if" we should have to parachute, but "when." It was a sobering thought, and we started to take the instructors more seriously.

One of our pilots asked the inevitable question: "But what if the chute doesn't open and you just fall?" The parachute instructors had an answer for that one, too: "It's not the fall that hurts, it's that sudden stop at the end."

The important thing was to be prepared to bail out at anytime. When in combat, this meant keeping the harness straps pulled as tightly as possible, because to bail out with a loose harness could result in a dislocated arm or leg when the chute jerked open.

Bailing out of a Hellcat wasn't as simple as rolling back the canopy and jumping out. Do that and you would probably hit the tail. So, if you didn't want to have your top half go one way and the lower half another, the procedure was this: reduce airspeed to below 100 knots, roll back the canopy, unhook the radio and oxygen line, release shoulder straps and seat belt, roll the plane over so it's upside down, drop out of the cockpit and pull the D-ring of the ripcord.

Try that when you're burning up and the Japs are shooting you full of holes!

Being a poor swimmer, if I had to bail out I would prefer doing it over land. But if I had to bail out over water I was prepared. This is what I was taught to do: as soon as the parachute blossoms open, unclasp the leg straps, and keeping elbows tucked in close, unclasp the chest strap, then sit back into the swinglike seat of the harness. Just before hitting the drink, throw your arms up and slide out of the harness. The life raft is thethered to the Mae West by a lanyard. This way the chute falls forward, and since there is no drag, it collapses. You then swim over to the liferaft pack, tear it open and inflate the raft by pulling the toggle of the $CO_2$ bottle. After that, climb into the raft and wait for a float plane or submarine to pick you up.

Sounded simple enough to me.

# 9

# *Harder* on Patrol

ABOARD THE SUBMARINE, U.S.S. *HARDER* (SS 257), IN THE SOUTHWEST PACIFIC, MARCH 29, 1944.

"Woleai!" shouted the high periscope lookout, not turning his eyes away. "Distance fifteen miles, sir."

Lieutenant Frank C. "Tiny" Lynch, the sub's six-foot-five bulk of an executive officer, and the other men in the control room glanced first at the lookout, then at the man who was leading them on their fourth combat patrol, Commander Samuel David Dealey, of Dallas, Texas.

Commander Dealey checked his watch—0715, right on schedule. Like the coach of a winning football team, he was proud of his men, and there wasn't another command he'd rather have.

With determination glistening in his gold-specked brown eyes, Sam Dealey took over at the periscope, grasping a familiar handle with one hand, while wrapping his other arm around the polished brass shaft and nuzzling his face against the soft rubber eye-piece.

Through the sharply focused lens of the periscope, Dealey's keen eyes studied the distant atoll's outline on the horizon. The sealed orders he had opened right after leaving Pearl Harbor gave him only scanty information about Woleai. Lying on the southern tip of the atoll, Woleai was the largest island, which gave the cluster of twenty or more jungle infested reefs their name. The islands were strung together in a figure eight, on the side opposite the *Harder* they formed a large lagoon capable of anchoring fuel tankers and supply ships.

According to Sam Dealey's information, Woleai's dense jungle probably hid a newly constructed Jap airstrip. From there, Zero fighters and medium-class Betty bombers could strike against America's encroaching Pacific Fleet, thus protecting their island strongholds. This included Truk, 500 miles north, and stretched 400 miles south to New Guinea.

Dealey's orders were twofold. First, he was to locate the hidden airfield and confirm its existence to Vice Admiral Charles A. Lockwood, Commander, Submarines, Pacific Fleet. The second part of Dealey's mission was to join the Lifeguard League and station the *Harder* off the shore of Woleai. Operating under the lifeguard code name "Falstaff," the *Harder* was to stand by to rescue any zoomies who might get shot down or for some other reason be forced to ditch their planes at sea.

"Contact! Radar contact with Woleai, sir," called out the radar operator. "Range 29,600 yards, sir."

Dealey nodded in acknowledgment, and the *Harder* continued steady on course for Woleai.

Admiral Lockwood later wrote in his history of the *Harder, Through Hell and Deep Water*: "As usual, Dealey was heading for a very hot area, but this time he was far removed from the fragrant shores of Honshu [Japan] where he had made his first three patrols."[1]

The *Harder's* crew had gained confidence in their captain during the successful American assaults on the islands of

Tarawa, Makin, Apamama, and the entire Gilbert Islands group. Sam Dealey had led his crew in sinking three Jap freighters and damaging another one on November 19 and 20. Days later, on their second patrol, they sank four ships and damaged one.

Those first three patrols had earned Dealey and his crew the respect of the Navy, and the *Harder* was reverently known throughout the Pacific as the *submarine of submarines.*

While Dealey was ever mindful of the safety and well-being of his crew and boat, he also realized the broader responsibility of carrying out his mission in contributing to the overall success of Admiral Raymond A. Spruance's Fifth Fleet.

In what was the largest amphibious operation yet undertaken, the Marshall Islands had been secured, thanks to the Fifth Fleet's heavy air and sea shelling, which prepared for assaults by army and marine divisions.

Next came the taking of the Kwajalein Atoll, the abandoned Majuro Island and Eniwetok on February 20, which gave the Fleet three new strategic anchorages.

And now the *Harder* was to keep an eye on Woleai and assume lifeguarding duties as part of a massive, impending strike by the Fifth Fleet against the Western Caroline Islands. The strike was planned to destroy the enemy airbases at Palau, Yap and Woleai, in order to set the stage for General Douglas MacArthur's advance up the northern New Guinea coast.

The spearhead of the assault force was the Fast Carrier Task Force Fifty-Eight, with its sixteen aircraft carriers, under the command of Vice Admiral Marc A. Mitscher, operating from the carrier *Lexington.*

At 0815, March 29—a scant hour after the *Harder* first sighted Woleai, the lookout spotted an enemy aircraft taking off from the island.

Sam Dealey was elated over the discovery, but his immediate response was to take quick evasive action, just in case the plane might turn in the *Harder's* direction. "Dive!" he shouted.

114

"Take her down to eighty feet."

Within seconds, the *Harder* had slipped quietly below the surface and well out of sight of any nosey Nip pilot. The sub continued on course, submerged, with Dealey's keen eyes rivited to the periscope.

After reaching a point two miles from Woleai, the *Harder* slowly cruised the shallow waters parallel to the shoreline. Six times that day, Jap planes were observed landing or taking off. Whenever a plane flew too close to the *Harder*, Dealey initiated the usual evasive tactic: dive...stay submerged for an hour...rise to periscope depth...and, if no planes were seen, surface, recharge batteries and continue observation.

In an attempt to see the airstrip, Dealey gradually maneuvered the *Harder* in as close to shore as safety allowed. No luck. The jungle hid everything.

Then, on a hunch, he sailed around to the lagoon side of Woleai. As the *Harder* glided silently beneath the surface into the lagoon, Dealey panned the area with the periscope and was satisfied that no ships were in port. He turned the periscope over to Frank Lynch, and maneuvered the sub to within a half-mile of shore.

Moments later Lynch sighted the air strip. It was about 3000 feet long, and a Betty bomber was poised at one end, preparing for take-off. Dealey's hunch had paid off.

The next day only two aircraft were spotted some distance away. It was hardly anything to get excited about. This was monotonous duty, but Dealey's surviellance of the island and his report of the new air strip gave the Navy just the intelligence information they needed.

March 31 and April 1 were days to look forward to. According to Dealey's information, Allied planes would be sent in then to wipe any trace of the Japs from the face of the island. The plan was to send high level Army B-17 Flying Fortress bombers on March 31, followed on April 1 with a half-day of strikes by carrier planes from Admiral Mitscher's Fast

Carrier Task Force Fifty-Eight, part of Admiral Spruance's Fifth Fleet.

The Army's B-17s hit the Japs while they slept—at 0105 the morning of March 31, and took them so much by surprise that there had been no anti-aircraft fire from the ground. Dealey watched through the periscope as the Flying Fortresses bombed everything in sight—parked planes, vehicles, buildings and supply dumps.

Seven minutes later the second wave attacked, but this time the Japs were wide awake and manning their guns.

The third bombing came at 0200. The Japs were really getting a beating, but they persistently hung on and later were able to get some planes back into the air. It amazed Dealey that anything was left intact on the island, following the devastating attacks by the Army bombers. His log revealed no American airplane losses, which meant no downed zoomies to pluck from the sea.

Throughout the day the *Harder* spotted enemy aircraft flying over and around the island—a number of land-based bombers and an occasional float-type scout plane that persistently plied the coastal areas in search of American submarines.

At 0950, while lowering the periscope after spotting a Nip scout plane, an aircraft bomb exploded close to the sub. Dealey entered in his log that the bridge talk-back was knocked out of order, several light bulbs were shattered and the ship was well shaken up. But there was no *serious* damage.

The *Harder* made a successful dive to 100 feet and escaped. For the rest of the day, the boat ran at eighty feet, planing up to periscope depth every fifteen minutes.

# 10

# Target: Woleai

ABOARD THE U.S.S. *BUNKER HILL* April 1, 1944.

*Bong-bong-bong....*

"Now hear this...all pilots, report to your ready rooms," the squawkbox ordered.

Routed out of my bunk at three in the morning. What a way to start the day. Peedy Boyles was saying just last night that after two days of combat missions we should be getting April Fool's Day off. That made sense to me, too. But we were wrong.

We frantically rushed to finish dressing, bumping into each other as we grabbed clothes from our narrow lockers that were squeezed together side-by-side.

I was already beginning to perspire heavily in the humid tropical air. We had no air conditioning on the *Bunker Hill*, except in the pilots' ready rooms and the Combat Information Center, which was deep in the bowels of the ship. We did have a fresh air vent, but it only helped when I was in my bunk. This was because Peedy had tied a pair of trousers to the vent, with one leg aiming a stream of air at himself in the upper bunk and the other toward me in the lower one. It was a sacrifice we had to make, because now there was no air hitting us in front of our lockers.

I swept the curtain aside that served as a door to our compartment, and, with Peedy close on my heels, spilled into the crowded light green passageway and ran with the others to an open catwalk on the side of the carrier. We scurried up two flights of ladders to the ready room, which was one deck below the flight deck. There were men running every which way, and while it seemed confusing, every one of the 3000 officers and enlisted men had specified jobs to do and knew exactly where they were headed.

Within minutes all pilots of VF-8 were assembled and seated in the ready room, and curling cigarette smoke was filling the place with a gray haze. I retrieved my plotting board and oxygen mask from under my leather reclining chair, then glanced at my peg on the bulkhead. My gear was all there—zoot suit, parachute harness and Mae West.

I told myself to remember to check the $CO_2$ cartridges in the Mae West. Sometimes they would be missing. Occasionally a sailor helped himself and used them for mixing "$CO_2$ cocktails." You wouldn't believe the ingredients!—alcohol from torpedoes mixed with a little glycol (which is used in the water injection systems in our fighters), then charged with $CO_2$ from our Mae Wests. I never tasted the brew because I heard it could cause blindness or death. Besides, they said it gave quite a kick and one super hangover. I had to be sure that if I needed my Mae West there would be $CO_2$ cartriges to inflate it.

Commander Collins, our squadron's skipper, gave us our briefing. "You're going in to attack Woleai Atoll, because we're going to be retiring by this little place," he smiled, intending his remark to instil some humor into the briefing. After no one cracked a smile, he abandoned the attempt at being a comic, cleared his throat and continued in a more serious vein: "Actually, it's a stepping stone between Truk Island and New Guinea."

I hung on every word he said, and the excitement and anticipation of my fifth combat mission charged my veins with adrenalin. The other pilots felt the same way. As eyes met around the room, there were a few anxious smiles. Some of the boys squirmed out of nervousness. The briefing turned into more of a pep-talk, and it reminded me of my high school coach talking to the guys in the locker room minutes before a football game.

After Collins finished the briefing, we went down to the officers' wardroom for breakfast. It was a huge compartment, capable of seating 700 men. The ship's officers as well as air group officers had their meals there. I always felt a little out of place, especially when I wore my khaki flight suit. But now only pilots were in the wardroom, and all of us were dressed that way.

Unlike the enlisted men's noisy and very functional cafeteria-style mess hall, the wardroom was quiet and formal—white, starched linen table cloths, real silverware and expensive china and crystal. We were served by black or Filipino stewards dressed in white linen jackets. Dad was right about the Navy being high-class for an officer.

Unfortunately, the food did not live up to the formality of the place—or to Dad's expectations. Ugh! Who could stomach horse meat and powdered eggs at that ungodly early time of day? But that's all there was to eat.

As I shoved the chow back away from me, a Catholic chaplain—a lieutenant maybe thirty-five, sitting across from me, said, "You know, the Navy doesn't give you steak and eggs in the morning just to be nice—it's an old Navy custom. They do it when you are going into battle, because you might not eat again that day!"

120

*Not this cookie*, I thought. *Who needs some guy with his collar on backwards to tell me what and when to eat!* My temper flared, but I kept the lid on. No way would I eat after *that.*

"Attention all pilots," droned the squawkbox. "Get the latest poop on the teletype screen...."

The teletype screen was mounted on a bulkhead in the ready room. It indicated the wind course and speed, ship's course and speed, heading and distance to the target, homing device frequency and call letters, and squadron flight frequency. The final information was the frequency of Falstaff, the lifeguard submarine.

Next came the intelligence briefing on the target. We studied some out-dated maps from World War I (the latest available), and were told how many Jap planes to expect and the estimated number of anti-aircraft guns in the vicinity.

Everything we needed to know was communicated before the takeoff because there could be no use of radios in flight except during actual combat or some other emergency. This was to keep the Japs from locating us by intercepting our transmissions and eavesdropping on our conversations. But if I did need to use the radio, the code words were: "Tiger Base" for the carrier and "Tiger Seven-One" for my flight leader—Gus.

In the air we relied on a visual Morse code for communications among pilots. A fist was a "dot" and an open palm a "dash."

With the briefing out of the way and our mission plotted, all there was left to do was to sit and wait for the squawkbox to announce...

"Pilots, man your planes!"

Everyone sprang into action. Hearing that command always ran a chill up my spine. What a thrill!

Just outside the ready room was a convenient head for the Nervous Jervice to toss his cookies before heading up to the flight deck. Not that there was anything disgraceful about it. The excitement and anticipation got to some of the best of pilots.

Stooped over and waddling along in my cumbersome flight gear and too-tight parachute harness, I clambered along the catwalk and up a ladder to the flight deck. The carrier was blacked out so as not to attract any snoopy Nip scout planes, and finding my assigned plane in the dim pre-dawn wasn't easy.

The flight deck was alive with activity. Our F6Fs, wings folded back, were jammed close together to conserve space. The planes were already fueled and armed with bombs and belts of .50-caliber ammo for the machine guns. The deck crews, with different colored skull caps and T-shirts to identify whether they were plane handlers, mechanics, or whatever, were swarming over the planes like ants on a log, tending to last minute preparations for take-off.

With the help of a mechanic, I climbed into the snug cockpit and wedged down into the deep bucket seat. I stowed the plotting board, hooked up my harness to the parachute, connected the oxygen line, fastened seat belts and shoulder straps, and then began the pre-flight check.

Whatever conversation there was with my mechanic was briefly functional and fast forgotten, because my mind was on the mission and nothing else.

No sooner did I complete the pre-flight check, than the squawkbox blared, "Pilots, stand by to start engines.... Stand clear of propellers!"

Most of the deck crew cleared the area, leaving only a few plane handlers to assist with the actual launch—and they darted to the designated safe spot under the planes.

"Pilots, start your engines!" ordered the squawkbox, with a slightly detectable hint of emotion.

I pressed the starter and the Grumman's engine grudgingly turned over, coughing and belching white smoke from its

throaty exhaust pipes. It caught, and I advanced the throttle
with my left hand.

All instruments—check.

Set gyros—check.

Then a faint *beep* came over my earphones, which was a
signal to indicate the radio was working.

The thundering roar of all those Hellcats was deafening.
White, acrid exhaust smoke swirled in the grey dawn. In
moments I smelled the smoke as it blended in with the odor
of my engine's hot oil and the rubber scent of my oxygen
mask. Airplane exhaust had a bite to it that I always imagined made my nostrils flare like a thoroughbred's. There were
other symptoms also—rapid pulse and fast, heavy breathing.
What a facade of confidence, sitting at the controls of that
Hellcat. It made me feel like a man of steel—like Superman

himself. I'm not proud to say that right then I had more faith in Grumman than God.

Up on the bridge, Admiral Montgomery gave the order for the entire fleet to head into the wind so the carriers could launch their planes. As the *Bunker Hill* turned into the wind, a stiff breeze swept across the flight deck.

Moments later the first Hellcat was launched, and I soon lost sight of its faint silhouette in the pre-dawn darkness.

I sat there, awaiting my turn, worried, scared, apprehensive about the catapult, because you never get used to it. This was when my life flashed past in review.

Mom used to say, "If you are ever in trouble or afraid or need something, ask God for help, *believing* He will help you—and *He will!*"

I wasn't what you would call a religious person at the time, but I was scared, and I did have the Twenty-Third Psalm committed to memory, so I began reciting it—not so much because I thought God might actually be listening, but more to console myself:

"The Lord is my shepherd, I shall not want. He maketh me to lie down in green pastures; He leadeth me beside the still waters. He restoreth my soul; He leadeth me in the paths of righteousness for His name's sake. Yea, though I walk through the valley of the shadow of death, I shall fear no evil, for Thou art with me. Thy rod and Thy staff they comfort me. Thou preparest a table before me in the presence of mine enemies. Thou anointest my head with oil. My cup runneth over. Surely, goodness and mercy shall follow me all the days of my life. And I will dwell in the house of the Lord forever. Amen."

Other than reciting the Twenty-Third Psalm, it's difficult to remember what my thoughts were. I just concentrated on what I had to do.

Sitting somewhere in front of me, in the pitch black pre-dawn, was Gus' plane. I taxied up and came to within ten feet of him. Behind me came T.I. and Chris. Four men—division seven of VF-8, hopped up and fully charged, ready to dish it out to the Japs on Woleai.

Gus moved up to the catapult, and seconds later was shot off into the darkness. Then it was my turn.

There were two catapults—port and starboard. I released my brakes, eased the throttle forward and used my rudder to steer me to the starboard one. The catapult crew rushed into action and connected the catapult hook to the underside of my Hellcat.

Then came the eerie part. I had to release the brakes entirely and trust the hook to hold me. I advanced the throttle to catapult position—all the way forward. Full flaps, full power and *no* brakes.

The sweaty palm of my left hand rested against the throttle, but not gripping it, and my right was barely touching the stick. The catapult would force me back into the seat and I didn't want it to make me cut throttle and pull back on the stick. If I did, it would put me in a nose-high attitude with too little power to get into the air, and I'd end up in the drink for sure. That actually happened to some pilots in the early days, and the Navy lost some good men and planes until the procedure was corrected.

*How did the engine sound?* I asked myself. I had the last word on whether to take off. Any strange noise from the engine was justification for a shut down. The engine sounded fine. I gave an okay sign to Fly One, our flight officer. Over the squawkbox, I heard him give the command to catapult me.

Suddenly, the plane lurched forward, as the catapult sped toward the bow. The rapid acceleration caused me to sink back into my seat. The plane vibrated so hard that everything was a blur. I felt totally out of control.

Then, only 2.1 seconds and 110 feet later (as I recall from the training manual), I was airborne! The vibration stopped and the plane smoothed out at ninety knots. All was well, and I sighed a sigh of relief as I turned to join up with Gus.

# 11
# Fateful Impulse

Woleai Atoll would have remained a remote, obscure and mostly insignificant chain of tiny palm-studded islands in the deep South Pacific had the Japanese not embarked on their doomed mission of conquest. Troops were shipped in, then came the bulldozers, and a crude landing strip was gouged out of the dense jungle. Corrugated steel huts were erected, aviation fuel and other supplies stockpiled. The foreign sounds of heavy earth-moving equipment and the drone of Japanese medium bombers interrupted the more subtle sounds native to the now disturbed sanctuary of the islands—the sounds of birds and insects and a few species of monkeys and other jungle animals.

Near the landing strip—at the end where planes parked temporarily to prepare for take-off, the fronds of palm trees that once swayed in the balmy tropical breeze were now tattered and shredded from the harsh wind-blast of aircraft propellers. They were omens of things to come. For the presence of the

Japanese military installation on Woleai was discovered by the U.S. Forces, and in quick order high-flying Army planes bombed the Japanese at least once and maybe twice, though little damage was inflicted on the Japanese and their facilities.

But April 1 was to be a day unlike any before on Woleai Atoll. This day the Japanese would get a pounding by Navy carrier planes.

The Navy command at Pearl Harbor kept our Fifth Fleet positioned a couple of hundred miles to the northwest of Woleai, standing by to launch its planes (mine included) for a pre-dawn attack, and the submarine *Harder*, code-named Falstaff, prowled to within fifty miles of the island, ready for lifeguard duty when the fireworks began.

I was never a superstitious person, so there was nothing portentous about April Fool's Day so far as I was concerned. It was going to be my third day of combat flying, and I was cocky and felt invincible.

Little did I know that on that particular April Fool's Day in 1944 I would do the most foolish thing of my life, setting into action a chain of events that even I wouldn't believe had I not experienced some and seen others. To me personally, it would be a lesson I would never forget.

For Sam Dealey and the crew of the *Harder*, April 1, 1944 would prove to be a day of unselfish daring, risk, bravery and heroism—all of which would only serve to perpetuate the growing legend about this sub skipper and his courageous crew.

Sam Dealey's first log entry on April 1 reveals that April Fool's day began early aboard the *Harder*. Shortly after midnight, the surface-search SJ radar picked up a hostile plane at 9500 yards. Dealey was peering over the shoulder of Warrant Officer Carl Finney, who was huddled behind the seated radar operator, at the blip on the radar screen. In seconds, the plane rapidly closed to only 6000 yards. The implication was obvious and immediate: the sub would have to take evasion action—*fast*!

"Dive!" shouted Dealey, "take her down to eighty feet!"

*Ahgoowa! ahgoowa!* the diving klaxon reverberated throughout the iron passageways and compartments of the submarine. It instantly triggered the release of adrenalin in every man's veins, because it was an all too familiar warning of impending danger—either an airplane attack or a destroyer's depth-charging.

The crew sprang into action.

Thanks to the skipper's insistence on many drills, each man attacked his assignment with the same "natural" instinct and aggressiveness as swatting a mosquito on his arm. Ship control men spun the large sprocketed wheels that opened the flood and vent valves, while others rotated the bow and stern planes to take her down quickly. The race was on to escape the fast approaching enemy plane.

The *Harder* vented its ballast tanks of air, spouting water into the air like a giant grey whale. Its slender nose dipped slightly downward, and the foaming sea rushed over the deck and churned against the side of the conning tower.

The last lookout cleared the bridge. Like most seasoned sailors, rather than climb down the ladder rung-by-rung, he gripped the smooth vertical pipes with both hands and both feet and, in a sliding shimmy, whisked down. He landed with a thump on both feet on the deck of the conning tower control room, then yanked down on the wire lanyard to latch the conning tower hatch. The heavy steel lid slammed closed, and the quartermaster spun down the hand wheel that dogged it shut, sealing the boat from the wave of sea water that spilled over the bridge.

The *Harder's* crack crew quietly and deftly carried out the operation which they had performed over a hundred times during their weeks at sea. In no more than a minute, the dive was accomplished and the sub glided silently beneath the surface, leaving only a trace of foam, which quickly dissolved as the surface of the water once again became calm.

Not knowing if they were successful in evading the Jap plane, the *Harder's* crew braced in anticipation of exploding depth charges.

Anxious seconds ticked away.

The men stood around in silent anticipation. At any moment a depth-charge could explode, ripping open the hull of the *Harder*, trapping her crew in a watery coffin, and sending her into the dark depths of Davy Jones' locker.

Some of the men's faces betrayed their thoughts and feelings. Tensed facial muscles. Locked jaws. Beads of sweat. There was no talking, only listening and bracing for what might happen.

Waiting for those explosions was never something a submariner got used to. There wasn't a man on board who didn't feel some apprehension. It quickened *everyone's* pulse!

No one appeared outwardly afraid. But inwardly? Who knows? No one lost control.

Sam Dealey, somber-faced and stern-jawed, was a model of composure.

All the men could do was wait and sweat it out.

The seconds ticked away. Still no explosions.

A few minutes went by. Tensions eased, and the men slowly began to relax.

After nearly two hours submerged, the *Harder* surfaced and proceeded to its assigned position near the lagoon. Sometime soon the carrier planes would arrive to launch a half-day of attacks on the atoll. Sam Dealey was supposed to be five miles northeast of Woleai's Point Option, but at the time of the attack was fifty miles south because he feared any planes in the area—including his own Navy's, whose pilots might mistake the *Harder* for a Jap sub.

At 0351, still in the black of night, radar picked up a Jap plane; its distance, 19,000 yards and closing. The men in the

*Harder's* control room kept their eyes glued to their Skipper, ready for him to give the command to dive. But Dealey held his ground, waiting until the last possible moment. The plane flew to within 14,000 yards, then turned. It evidentially never spotted the *Harder*.

Everyone breathed a little easier.

Time passed slowly. Hours went by. Dawn finally arrived, and the sky was clear of aircraft. Sam Dealey and his executive officer, Frank Lynch, had been up all night. They shared the same thoughts: *Where are our planes? When will the attack begin?*

At 0725 they got their answer. SJ radar picked up a flight of planes at 36,000 yards. Dealey scurried up the ladder to the bridge and squinted through binoculars, eagerly scanning the northern horizon for the planes. Fifteen minutes later, according to Admiral Lockwood's account, Dealey saw them—fighters, dive bombers and torpedo planes—heading straight for Woleai. Surely this airborne armada packed enough firepower to obliterate everything the Japs had on the island.

The morning breeze swept over the conning tower, carrying with it the distant din of scores of aircraft engines. It was going to be quite a show!

Dealey grinned as he watched the first wave of fighters peel off and dive toward the island's airstrip.

I was piloting one of those fighters. We didn't observe any ack-ack fire at first, and this only bolstered our hopes of catching the Japs by surprise. But what about tracers? They can't be seen when coming toward you—only after they have sped past. So I glanced back—and *saw* them! Hundreds of tracers were speeding away behind me.

Miraculously, I was flying through that deadly shower unscathed. But there wasn't time to think about anything but hitting a target, then hightailing it back up into the clouds, out of sight and range of the Jap's ack-ack guns.

*Hit something!* I told myself. Find a target.

Then I saw the Betty Bomber parked on the end of the runway, and that's when I did the most impulsive thing I had ever done in my life. I acted like one big April Fool!

I broke off from my formation and went after that bomber with all my guns blazing, despite what we had been taught and taught again—to stay together as a team.

And that's when the Japs riddled my Hellcat with exploding shells.

"Falstaff from Tiger Leader," Gus radioed the *Harder*.

The *Harder's* radio man, Ray Levin, answered the call.

"Fighter plane, burning, falling into the drink," Gus frantically called for help. "The pilot chuted out. He is now in the water—about five miles to the north of Taugalap...that's the second island west of Woleai."

Levin immediately passed the alert on to his skipper, and that's all Dealey needed to hear. He turned the periscope over to Lynch, then slid down the ladder to the main control room where the navigation charts were spread out on a plotting board.

Dealey hovered over the chart and quickly plotted the shortest course to my location. It would take the sub around the northeast corner of Woleai. He set a new course northward. "Full speed!" he called out.

The Officer of the Deck rang the command down to the engine room. The *Harder* turned to the north and began picking up speed, slicing through high waves in the rough sea, sending rooster tails spraying into the breeze. Lynch periodically cut in, giving Sam the ship's position by periscope bearings.

The same thought nagged at each man's consciousness: Would the *Harder* get there in time?

"The race to save a life was on," wrote Admiral Lockwood, who was monitoring the *Harder's* movements from his war room at Pearl Harbor.

## Salvation for a Doomed Zoomie

I was injured and exhausted after being buffeted around by the merciless sea. I was aware of three Hellcats circling overhead, and assumed they were piloted by Gus, T.I. and Chris. By now, I was confident that Gus had reported my position to Falstaff and the *Bunker Hill*. Good ol' Gus!

But there was no submarine in sight. Where was it? *C'mon, you guys, hurry up, before I drown or the sharks get me!*

I had visions of seeing this big, beautiful sub surface only yards away from where I was bobbing around, making a miserable attempt to swim and stay afloat. The crew scrambles onto the deck and someone throws a line to me. I retrieve it, hang on and get plucked out of the sea. That's how I envisioned my rescue. But I saw nothing. *Where* was *that sub*?

Then doubt began to gnaw at me again. What if Gus and T.I. and Chris *didn't* see me? What if they hadn't seen my parachute? What if they thought I went down with my Hellcat? Surely the sub would check out the vicinity, just in case...wouldn't it? But what if Gus *didn't* radio the sub? What if the Navy goofed? What if through some snafu there wasn't a sub in the area? But it *had* to be there! *My God! I'm desperate!* In order to keep from totally panicking, I *had* to have faith that Falstaff was cruising in the immediate vicinity.

In reality Falstaff was miles and miles out, racing to get to me before I fell victim to the sea, the sharks or the Japs. It was going to be close.

As I pondered all this, I was unaware that I was drifting with the wind and tide toward shallow water and dangerous coral reefs.

Unknown to me, at that moment aboard the *Harder*, Sam Dealey hurriedly plotted my rescue, realizing he was in a frantic race against time. Admiral Lockwood's documentary captures the urgent intensity of those desperate minutes:

"Studying the chart he had brought to the bridge, Sam saw that the downed flyer must be drifting toward the island of

Tagaulap, a...strip of sand and coral covered by dense jungle vegetation. Further checking the chart, he found that fairly deep water, twenty fathoms or better, reached almost to the reef that skirted the shoreline 1500 yards off shore. If the man survived until Sam could reach him, there might be a good chance of picking him up—provided, of course, Jap opposition didn't make it impossible for the sub to stay on surface. Naturally, in-shore work could be highly dangerous if the *Harder* were caught in shallow water by enemy planes. It could be the end for the sub and all hands. But if such thoughts passed through the skipper's mind, he kept them well concealed. He probably calculated his risks, as he always did, and figured that the Jap planes would have other problems to worry about. It would take all of three hours to make the run, even at full speed, around the east coast of Woleai to the spot where the aviator was reported down."[2]

*Three hours* to reach me? Had I known the sub was that far away, I surely would have given up the struggle. Sam Dealey knew the odds too, but being the unwavering sub skipper that he was, he pressed on for the rescue with total faith and confidence that he would arrive in time. The drama from the *Harder's* viewpoint was told by Dealey in the pages of the sub's log. Void of sensational adjectives, the matter of fact account is worded in the typically modest style of this unassuming, mild-mannered tiger of the Pacific:

"0840—Made full speed on four engines. From here on, the picture in the skies looked like a gigantic Cleveland Air Show. With dozens of fighters forming a comfortable umbrella above us, we watched a show that made the Hollywood colossals seem tame. We rounded the southeast coast of Woleai one to two miles off the beach and had the perfect ringside seat.

"The plastering that the airmen gave this Jap base was terrific! Bombs of all sizes rained on every structure on the island.

Several buildings seemed to be lifted and thrown high in the air. Causeways between the various islands were bombed. Oil or gasoline storage tanks blew up, covering the islands with heavy clouds of black smoke. The runway on the island was hit time and again with large and small bombs. It was hard to believe that anything could be left on the islands after the first waves of planes had gone over, and yet some bursts of anti-aircraft fire continued to meet the planes on each attack.

"The bombers hit Woleai from the south, waited for the smoke to clear, reformed, and then gave it the works from east-west courses! Fighters seemed to hit the place from all directions, peeling off from high above and diving straight into the ack-ack fire that still persisted. Many looked as if they would go right on through the blanket of smoke and crash on the islands, but all managed to pull out just above the trees. Fires blazed intermittently on Woleai and most of its adjacent islands, and gradually the anti-aircraft defense was reduced to a few sporadic bursts."[3]

Hours later, after I had miraculously made my way to the beach, I was buzzed out of my siesta on the sand when a TBM torpedo bomber thundered by no more than ten feet over my head. But I didn't move. The TBM made several more low passes over me, and I finally rolled over and sat up. The plane circled back and buzzed me again. This time, seeing that I was alive, he wagged his wings and dropped what resembled a large bean-bag with a red streamer. The bundle hit the sand and bounced a few times, coming to rest only a few yards away. Somehow I mustered enough strength to crawl over to it.

Inside I found a written message. With shaky hands I unfolded the note and read: "Swim out to sea, Falstaff is coming!"

*What? You gotta be kiddin'!* I thought.

After four and a half hours in the water my arms and legs were like rubber, and I wasn't about to go back into the ocean!

Sounds crazy now, but that's truthfully what I thought at the time.

The *Harder* was one mile off the northeast corner of Woleai when the replacement fighters from Admiral Spruance arrived. The planes zoomed the sub and guided it toward my location on the beach.

Sam Dealey scanned the beach through his binoculars, hoping to spot a sheltered cove or anchorage where the deep-draft sub could enter to pick me up. But all he saw was shallow water and a narrow, sandy beach. He was faced with only one alternative: he would have to bring the sub all the way to shore.

According to the *Harder's* log, at 1145 Dealey finally sighted me "on the northwest tip of the second island to the west of Woleai." The log entry went on to give details of the sub's approach: "Battle surface stations were manned, the ship was flooded down and maneuvered into a spot about 1500 yards off the beach. White water was breaking over the shoals only twenty yards in front of the ship and the fathometer had ceased to record."

I'll never forget the spectacle of seeing that sub coming directly toward me. What a sight! It looked big enough to be a destroyer. But I couldn't understand it: how could a sub rescue me off the beach?

Still the sub came closer and closer to shore.

*Are they going to drive that up on the beach for me? They're crazy!*

Then I saw something that almost made my heart stop beating. At first I wasn't sure, but then I knew that...*the sub was backing away!*

"Please, God, don't let them leave! I'll swim. I'll get there. Why do they leave me after all this?" And I guess I caved in.

During all of this, I was unaware of another drama unfolding. The *Harder's* log shows that one of the circling planes advised the sub that if rescue looked too difficult from its location, a better approach might be made from another direction.

The *Harder's* Skipper looked the situation over, then decided to go for the alternate approach. He proceeded to back off, with the intention of coming back in from another angle. He wrote in the log that he had seen me standing on the beach, then fall and lie there outstretched on the sand. My collapse, he speculated, "was undoubtedly due mainly to physical exhaustion, but also to the disappointment in seeing...chances of rescue fade away."

He was correct. And how!

Then, in a crazy change of events, one of the search planes reported to Dealey that the first approach was best after all. I saw the sub reverse course and head back at full speed in my direction.[4] They were coming back! A new hope surged through my veins.

# 12

# Salvation at Sea

The lookouts on the *Harder's* bridge had plenty to watch. It was like trying to take in a three-ring circus all at once. I was in one "ring," the jungle in another, and the air attack in still another.

They were coming to rescue me, but seeing me as I lay death-like on the beach gave them some cause for concern. Was the person they saw alive or dead? Was he the American flyer they were looking for—or a clever Jap decoy?

They had every right to be skeptical because of my appearance. By this time I had no flight helmet and no Mae West, and my dark green G-suit looked black because it was dripping wet, looked black. My face didn't even look like an American's. It was too dark. How could they know it was from a blistering sunburn covered with dried blood (from being grated over the coral)?

Added to the confusing scenario before them was a *second* man who looked like he might be an island native. Squatting on the beach only a short distance away from where I lay, he was calmly watching all that was going on. His presence made the men of the *Harder* even more wary of a trap. Was he really a native? Or a Jap in disguise? If he was a native, was he friendly? Did he have friends hiding out at the edge of the jungle, just waiting for the sub to move into a trap? I didn't even know he was there.

Now the sub's lookouts had all the more reason to scan "ring two"—the dense jungle's edge where it met the sand of the beach. They had to scruitinize every suspect little shadow, straining their eyes to see any possible tell-tale signs of men in hiding.

In the "third ring" of this unlikely circus was the sensational air attack over Woleai. But the lookouts weren't interested in being mere spectators; they kept a watchful eye in the event a Zero might appear on the scene. As it turned out not a single Jap plane got into the air—thanks to my buddies up there in those beautiful Hellcats!

Gus, T.I. and Chris continued circling overhead as the *Harder* eased in closer to shore. I couldn't hear them talking to me, of course, but I sensed they were praying for me not to give up.

Meanwhile, their gas gauges were going down, down and *down*! They would soon have to return to the carrier. But without air cover, what would happen to me? Were the Japs just waiting for the planes to leave so they could safely come after me? And what would happen to the *Harder* without air cover? It would also be at the mercy of the Japs. Was the risk in trying to rescue me too great? Maybe the *Harder* should abort the attempt!

Those were the considerations Sam Dealey had to deal with, and being the man of faith that he was, he no doubt prayed, seeking God's wisdom and divine guidance and protection. To this indomitable sub skipper there was only one thing to do: he sent an urgent message to Admiral Spruance. It read:

"Prolong the attack and provide air cover and we will effect the rescue."

Gus had already radioed the admiral to send in more air support to cover my rescue, and now Dealey asks him to prolong the attack! Put this into prospective for a moment: There was Admiral Spruance, commanding the entire Fifth Fleet—110 ships, including sixteen aircraft carriers, and he is asked to do all these things for the sake of rescuing a single pilot whose foolishness got himself shot out of the sky!

Unbelievable! Unheard of! Prolong the fleet for one, solitary man? It was crazy! Would Tojo have approved such a request? Would Hitler? Would Mussolini? Or Stalin? Of course not! A single life meant nothing to them! In their navies such "unmilitary" notions would surely have resulted in instant relief of command, probably followed by facing a firing squad or a short walk to the gallows!

My groggy, confused mind heard the drone of several more planes overhead. I looked up, and squinting into the brilliant tropical sun, made out the silhouettes of a handful of new carrier planes as they joined the formation of planes flown by Gus, T.I. and Chris. I figured they were replacement aircraft sent to keep an eye on me and to ward off any encroaching Japs. Three of the birds then broke off and headed east. No doubt my wingmates, now low on gas, were returning to their roosting place on the *Bunker Hill*.

Meanwhile, the sub was inching in closer to shore. Brave men were trying to save my life, and all I was doing was resting on the sand. I didn't know what I could do to help, but I had to do *something*!

Though my battered body was numb all over, I struggled to my feet and tried to wade out into the surf to meet the incoming sub. I was knee-deep in the boiling surf when a breaker hit me, causing my wobbly legs to buckle. The powerful wave tumbled and rolled me across the bottom. Caught in a flood of sandy seawater foam, I was washed back up onto the beach.

A new surge of pain gripped my body and I passed out. Moments later, I opened my eyes and lay on the beach, panting for breath and hoping for a resurgence of strength. I *had* to reach that sub! But my muscles were as useless as wet noodles. I couldn't move.

Groggy as I was, I heard our planes as they swooped over the island and strafed and bombed the airstrip, keeping the Jap's anti-aircraft batteries busy. Blinking sand and sea-water from my burning eyes, my vision was blurry as I strained to focus on the jungle, fully expecting at any moment to see a hoard of Japs run out of the trees, guns ablazin'.

I slowly and painfully turned my head in the direction of the sub. It hardly seemed to be moving, it was going so slowly.

*Can't you guys speed that thing up!*

But the sub was in shallow waters inundated by a myriad of hardened coral heads that could rip open a boat's hull, and the going had to be slow and cautious. By now the sub was a sitting duck, no longer in water deep enough to dive for safety.

How long would it be before the Japs discovered the vulnerable sub and come after it? Ground fire could inflict serious damage, and a Zero could sink it with a single bomb. But how could there be any Jap planes around? It seemed impossible that anything could be left intact on the island after the beating our planes were giving it.

Our airmen weren't just about to let the Japs get close enough to get off a single shot at the *Harder*, or at me. Sam Dealey needed time to maneuver the sub in closer for the rescue, and our boys in the air were bound and determined to give him all the protection he needed. I had a lot of confidence in those guys, and knew they were the best trained pilots in the world—and to think they were up there, risking their necks because I impulsively went after that Jap bomber and got myself shot down.

ENSIGN GALVIN ANXIOUSLY WATCHING APPROACH OF U.S.S. HARDER. TO COVER THIS APPROACH AND THE SUBSEQUENT RESCUE THE AIR FORCE PUT OVER A COMFORTABLE UMBRELLA OF PLANES, TO QUOTE THE COMMANDING OFFICER IT LOOKED LIKE A "CLEVELAND AIR SHOW" AND THE PLASTERING THAT THE AIR MEN GAVE THIS JAP BASE WAS TERRIFIC!

U.S. Navy photo by Air Group Commander Andrew Jackson

The activity on the *Harder* during this time was months later reported in a Navy magazine—the *Information Bulletin*, published by the Bureau of Naval Personnel. According to that story, Sam Dealey was preparing to send a rescue squad for me. He ordered some of the crew to make ready the rubber boat. But through some snafu, there were no paddles aboard, and the men would have to paddle with their hands.

Dealey called for volunteers and explained the risk involved.

"I want you to know," he said, "if you go in there, heavy fire from the shore may force us to cut away and back down—and we may not be able to come back after you."

He paused, searching the men's eyes as his appraisal of the risky mission sunk in. Each man was weighing the possible consequences of volunteering. To step forward would require tremendous courage—far and above the normal call of duty.

AVIATOR WAS TOO EXHAUSTED TO COME THROUGH THE SURF.
THREE MEN WERE SELECTED, LT. SAM LOGAN,"J""W" THOMASON
SCIc, AND F.X.RYAN, MoMMIc, FROM A LARGE GROUP OF
VOLUNTEERS TO SWIM IN AND GET HIM OUT, A DISTANCE
OF ABOUT 1200 YARDS.

U.S. Navy photo by Air Group Commander Andrew Jackson

"And another thing," Dealey added, breaking the uneasy silence, "the Japs may be setting a trap, just waiting for more men to get farther in."[1]

Then Dealey called for those who wanted to volunteer. Practically the *whole crew* stepped forward! The slight smile that escaped Dealey's face scarcely betrayed the swelling pride in his heart for his men. He would have to make a selection. He singled out the crew's three best swimmers. Lieutenant Samuel M. Logan, a brilliant Kentuckian, who was number one in his graduating class at Annapolis, was chosen to head the rescue squad. The other two were J. W. Thomason, twenty-four, a ship's cook first class from Danielsville, Georgia, and Francis X. Ryan, twenty, a motor-machinist mate first class from Shenandoah, Pennsylvania.

As the three men prepared to board the rubber boat and come after me, Sam Dealey turned his attention to maneuvering the sub into shore as closely as possible. He directed Frank Lynch to be personally responsible for supervising the engine room during the tricky maneuver. Dealey skillfully inched the sub closer and closer to shore, until its bow eventually scraped into the coral bottom, and Lynch saw that the slow-moving screws kept the *Harder's* nose on the reef and helped prevent the stern from turning the sub parallel to shore. Unless the job was handled with great skill, the sub would drift broadside against the crashing waves, washing the boat helplessly onto the beach.

It was an unnatural spot for a submarine to be in, and no one on board felt easy about it, especially Lynch. For him, the ordeal was sheer, unadulterated agony. The sub's bow was riding high on the reef while the stern churned up white water. Each wave raised the sub's stern, sending the bow deeper and causing it to bump and grind on the reef. Everytime this happened, the clanging and banging echoed throughout the sub. To the crewmen inside, nervously sweating out the rescue and unable to see what was happening, it sounded as if the sub was about to break up. Several members of the crew later confessed they thought their skipper was a bit too daring, nevertheless they had unwavering confidence in him.

The words of Lieutenant Commander Edward Beach, which years later appeared in *The Blue Book* magazine, best describe Sam Dealey in that momentous hour:

"A man of firm decision, enterprising character, brilliant and forceful of execution, Commander Sam D. Dealey now resolved deliberately to run *Harder* aground, in order to expedite the rescue. With her bow well flooded down, nearly six feet deeper in the water forward, he anticipated no great difficulty in getting her off after blowing the tanks again. Closer and closer to the menacing surf moved the submarine, proceeding very slowly, so as to receive the minimum damage

U.S. Navy photo by Air Group Commander Andrew Jackson

upon striking. In the control room the fathometer was running continuously, and finally it simply ceased to record because the bottom was too close. Shortly after this the men in the forward torpedo room, who had been ordered to report as soon as the ship hit bottom, heard a scraping noise beneath the keel. *Harder* was aground!"[2]

Just before noon the three volunteers dove over the side and started pushing and towing their rubber boat toward the beach, about 1200 yards away. A line was played out from the sub to the rubber raft in order to pull it back from the beach.

From my vantage point, I could see every gun on the *Harder* aimed in my direction. They stayed trained on me throughout the course of the rescue, obviously in the event I turned out to be bait for a trap.

## Salvation for a Doomed Zoomie

LIFE RAFT DROPPED TO ENSIGN GALVIN BY PLANE

While the three men slowly made their way in the rubber boat toward shore, one of our planes dropped a rubber boat to me. It landed in the water only a few yards away from where I lay, and somehow I found the strength to crawl over to it, though the entire right side of my body was paralyzed and totally useless by now. I yanked the $CO_2$ toggle and the raft quickly inflated. I was in great pain, and it took considerable effort, but I managed to crawl into the surf, dragging the rubber boat with a tether line. I pulled myself over the boat's slippery rubber shoulder and slid into the bottom.

Oh, I was exhausted! But there was no time to rest.

One-man rafts came with no oars since they were not intended for travel, but simply to keep an occupant afloat. Yet I needed to *travel*!—all the way out to the waiting sub. I'd just have to lie in the raft and paddle with my hands—and

148

they barely reached the water. It was almost a futile effort, but I hastily started paddling as best I could out to sea in the direction of the sub. I was headed into the wind and going against the current, and several times I spun around in a circle, getting nowhere fast.

What was a bane to me was a blessing to the rescue party. The wind and current were actually helping them by floating their rubber boat directly toward me. The line connecting the rescue boat to the sub paid out, fortunately at a point where they could touch bottom.

Sam Logan took Ryan with him and left Thomason with the rubber boat. The two men waded and swam through the rough surf toward me, cutting their feet and legs on the coral.

My rubber boat kept drifting parallel to shore, and my would-be rescuers were gaining little ground. I would have to abandon my raft and wait for them. I slid off into the water and clung onto a coral head to wait for my rescuers.

For about half an hour I watched as Logan and Ryan struggled through the surf. Finally they reached me. I was the happiest guy in the world, though the best I could do to show it was manage a weak smile.

My rescuers were almost as exhausted as I was, and their legs and feet were cut and bruised from being scraped over the coral. For them to volunteer to come for me was incredibly self-sacrificing. And for them to reach me took super-human strength and determination.

Just as their helping hands were getting me into their rubber boat, I heard a *plop* in the water and turned my head to see a splash only a few feet away. Then there were more *plops*. Snipers' bullets! We'd all been so busy we'd forgotten to keep an eye on the beach, and now the Japs had sneaked up and were taking pot-shots at us.

Logan waved frantically at the men on the deck of the *Harder*, signalling to them to begin pulling us back with the line. The men on the sub had also seen the bullets strike the water and answered with a burst of machine gun fire that ripped palm trees to shreds and kicked up sprays of sand. It was enough to send the Japs scurrying back into the jungle for cover.

Sam Dealey, one to take every precaution, immediately radioed the planes circling overhead to give us some cover. Our airmen were quick to oblige. They came in low over the water and strafed the edge of the jungle, surely killing some snipers and making the rest lie low until we got farther from the beach. When the planes pulled up to circle for another attack, the snipers resumed firing. Bullets whined over our heads and an occasional one plopped in the water near the rubber boat. They were shooting at the men on the bridge of the sub as well, and Dealey almost got a new part in his hair when one bullet, fired 1200 yards away, shot through his cap, barely missing his scalp! Fortunately for those of us in the water, there was a line attached to the little boat, and strong hands aboard the sub were pulling us to safety. With the current and wind against us, even with paddles, I doubt that the exhausted men could have rowed the boat back. It was a free ride, with 500 yards to go. I lay in the bottom of the boat, totally spent from the ordeal, while the others were in the water, swimming and guiding the boat toward the *Harder*. In a few minutes, I thought, we would be safely aboard the sub. Safety seemed so close, yet so far away.

Then a new problem developed.

One of the cruisers in the task force which had launched the air attack, heard that a flyer was down at sea off the coast of Woleai and sent a float plane to make the rescue. The plane arrived and landed on the water, evidentially intending to pick me up and take me back to my ship. The plane began taxiing toward us, but the pilot failed to see the vital line that stretched from our rubber boat to the sub.

Dealey and the men on the deck of the *Harder* saw the plane heading toward the line, and alarmed at what was about to

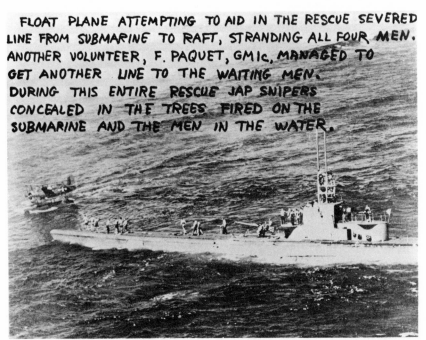

FLOAT PLANE ATTEMPTING TO AID IN THE RESCUE SEVERED LINE FROM SUBMARINE TO RAFT, STRANDING ALL FOUR MEN. ANOTHER VOLUNTEER, F. PAQUET, GM1c, MANAGED TO GET ANOTHER LINE TO THE WAITING MEN. DURING THIS ENTIRE RESCUE JAP SNIPERS CONCEALED IN THE TREES FIRED ON THE SUBMARINE AND THE MEN IN THE WATER.

U.S. Navy photo by Air Group Commander Andrew Jackson

happen, they waved and shouted to the pilot to look out for the line. But the pilot didn't comprehend.

On came the float plane, and it taxied right over the line, severing it with the sharp edge of its pontoon! Those of us in the rubber boat as well as the men on the sub stared incredulously at the parted line. My heart sank. My hope of rescue was growing dim.

But, as the story was later told to me, Sam Dealey wasted no time in swinging into action. He ordered the severed line hauled in and had one of the crew use a signal light to give directions to the rescue party. Thomason, the only man in the raft who wasn't too exhausted, swam back to the sub. Logan and Ryan guided our drifting raft to the reef nearest the *Harder* and hung on until we could be rescued.

In the few minutes since the line had been severed, our rubber boat had drifted until we were 800 yards from the *Harder*. To swim that distance in the rough sea and against the strong wind and current was a challenge for the best of swimmers. It would have been foolhearty for anyone less than an Olympic champion to even consider trying it. But without hesitation, Thomason jumped overboard and started swimming. He battled the thrashing waves and rushing current, and was gaining!

Meanwhile, Logan and Ryan paddled our raft to the reef, a distance of 1200 yards from the *Harder*. All we could do was wait.

Gunner's Mate Freeman Paquet Jr. volunteered to swim a new line out to us, but Sam Dealey, exercising sound caution, told him to wait in case Thomason should need help first. There was other reasoning behind Dealey's decision: the *Harder*, like most submarines, did not carry 1200 yards of line that was strong and light enough for a swimmer to carry and handle in a rough sea.

Agonizing minutes crept slowly by as the men on the sub shouted encouragement to Thomason as he struggled against the tossing waves.

Meanwhile, Dealey had a detail scour the sub for all the line it could find. The lighter-weight line that was originally attached to the rubber raft would be played out first, with the heavier scraps tied to it. Line of every size and description was hauled up to the deck. The last length was tied on as Thomason reached the hull of the sub.

Several of the crew precariously climbed down over the slippery side of the boat, clasping strong hands together to form a human chain. The man farthest down grabbed Thomason's outstretched hand and pulled him out of the water. Other crewmen helped haul him up to the deck.

Paquet's time had come. He dived over the side and began swimming the 1200 yards to where Logan, Ryan and I, still in our rubber boat, were clinging to a breaker-washed coral reef. He hastily tied the line to the raft and all hands on deck started hauling it in by hand, pulling all four of us in the rubber boat through the surf, against the wind and current, and finally along side of the boat.

I looked up at that sub and thought, *Man, that's a big turkey*! What a welcome sight!

Strong hands reached out to me and pulled me out of the rubber boat and onto the deck. I must have been semi-conscious, because I only vaguely remember being carried across the deck, up into the conning tower.

I was lowered through the hatch into the conning tower control room, and we all stopped to catch our breath. I just stood there, propped up by a couple of the crew. Every muscle in my body was spent, and I had a bad case of the shakes—from shock, I guess, not from the temperature of the air or water, because we were on the equator, and the air was hot and the water almost tepid. Weary and bleeding from cuts on my face, neck and hands, I was, oh, so grateful!

Everyone wanted to look me over, like I was a strange, soggy creature from Davy Jones' locker. The only thing that sagged more than my zoot suit was my bruised ego. One after another, the submariners filed by to look at the zoomie they had fished out. I felt like a circus freak, but I couldn't blame the crew for being curious.

Enough of the sideshow; they helped me into the captain's cabin and laid me on a bunk. One of them helped me out of my khaki flying jacket (why I still had that on, I don't know).

Curiosity got the best of them, and they kept firing questions at me, though I was in no condition to answer.

"What the hell is that you've got on?" asked someone, referring to my soggy zoot suit.

"What is it for?"

"How does it work?"

There I was, injured, bleeding and with one foot almost in the grave, and these jokers were only interested in my G-suit!

But that didn't last for long. One of the men seemed to be in charge, and his capable attention was reassuring. He was Pharmacist's Mate Angelo Lo Casio. (Subs had no doctors then, only hospital corpsmen.) With the help of another man, Angelo started to get me out of the wet suit, but the zippers were stuck because the fabric had shrunk so tightly. Someone came up with some scissors and they cut the suit away from my body. Two of the men hefted the heavy zoot suit.

"How did you swim with this?" asked one of them. They guessed it must have weighed twenty pounds! The air bags were filled or partially filled with water, and the heavy webbing had absorbed water like a sponge.

Someone in the Navy Department had really goofed, because they had not thought about the consequences to a pilot down at sea wearing that contraption. Besides the mistake of making the zoot suit out of heavy absorbant webbing, there was no check valve in the hose through which air passes to inflate the bladders. (Sam Dealey later sent off a choice-worded message to headquarters at Pearl Harbor about that one.)

Then off came my shoes—my good old, sturdy, dependable rugged field shoes. Why, they were so sodden with salt water they must have weighed two or three pounds—or more— apiece.

Someone produced some medicinal brandy to warm me up. Ouch! Did it sting at first! All the retching and salt water had made the lining of my mouth raw, and the brandy felt like a mouthfull of needles.

Next I was given a hot bath—which would be my last for ten days according to Angelo, because they had to conserve fresh water. Showers were only allowed when permitted by the chief engineer. "When I can't stand the smell of you guys," he was fond of saying, "then you can get a shower."

154

AVIATOR SAFELY ABOARD — ALL BACK FULL.

U.S. Navy photo by Air Group Commander Andrew Jackson

More than anything else, I needed to rest, so they helped me into Frank Lynch's bunk. But rest would not come for a while.

While Angelo had been tending to me, the *Harder* had reversed her engines and gently backed her nose off its unusual perch. One hour and twenty minutes after the rescue had begun, the sub was clear of the reef and headed out to sea.

Once in deep water, Dealey took the *Harder* down for a trim dive. Thirty minutes later, at 1630, the sub surfaced. Almost immediately, radar picked up a Jap bomber at a distance of nine miles and closing rapidly. It surprised Dealey because he felt certain that our carrier planes had demolished Woleai's airstrip, making it impossible for any Nip planes to take off.

But there was no time to think about that. Dealey ordered a crash dive that quickly took the *Harder* to a depth of 140 feet.

Just when I thought I was safe! There I was on that sub, just waiting for a depth charge to blast a hole in the hull and send us down to Davy Jones' locker for keeps.

But no bombs were dropped.

Dealey chose to stay under however until evening chow was over at 2030.

That night, Dealey recorded every detail of the rescue in the *Harder's* log. As could be expected of the sub's skipper, he made no mention of his own courageous contributions to my rescue, but instead cited the bravery of all the others involved:

"Throughout the entire rescue, the cooperation of the aviators was superb. They kept up a continuous pounding of the islands by bombs and flew in low to strafe the Japs and divert their attention from the rescue. In spite of this, Jap snipers concealed in the trees along the beach commenced shooting at the ship and rescue party and bullets whined over the bridge, uncomfortably close. The rescue could never have been attempted without the protection afforded by the planes. Too much praise cannot be given to the officer and the three [enlisted] men who effected this rescue. Its daring execution, under the noses of the Japs and subject to sniper fire from the beach, can be classified as a truly courageous accomplishment, and the rescued aviator—Ensign John R. Galvin— though physically exhausted, showed a character that refused to admit defeat. It is a privilege to serve with men such as these.

"This account has been written in considerable detail partly to portray the spectacular air smashing of a Jap base, and partly in sheer pride of the volunteers who carried out the rescue."[3]

Throughout the dramatic rescue Air Group Commander Andrew Jackson, accompanied by Jerry Rian in his plane, had been circling overhead in a photo F6F-3, recording the entire rescue operation on film.

Admiral Nimitz, a former submariner and Commander-in-Chief, Pacific Fleet, said he considered "the performance of the commanding officer, the officers and crew of the U.S.S. *Harder* one of the outstanding rescue feats accomplished to date in the Pacific area and in keeping with the high traditions of the entire submarine force.

"The cooperation between the attacking force and the rescue vessel is an example of a courageous fighting spirit and mutual support doctrine which will enable the Naval Service to overcome the greatest odds in successfully accomplishing its mission."[4]

Admiral Lockwood later wrote: "Neither Admiral Nimitz nor Commander Dealey took time out to interpret to the non-initiated what it means for a captain to put his ship into dreadful jeopardy by placing its nose on a reef to hold it in position while all hands risk their lives to save the life of one single nameless flyer—and willingly. Nor do they relate the deadly dangers that could develop by sudden attack from land, sea or air; nor the possibility that after a lapse of more than four hours, the zoomie might have been caught by skulking Japs and a Jap put in his place to act as bait to draw the submarine and its rescue crew into potentially dangerous water. So many things could have happened that it is nothing short of a miracle that none of them did."[5]

# 13
## Strange New World

In the dark recess of my mind I became aware of sounds. Whirring, humming, pumping. As I awakened further, the noises grew louder and more recognizable. They were the sounds of engines, fans and pumps, and of water and air passing through valves and lines. I felt the motion of the sub as it surged through the sea—gently rocking and swaying. I opened my eyes and squinted, trying to force them to focus in the dim red light that came from a lamp mounted on the bulkhead near the doorway.

I saw a wall-mounted clock. *Noon!* I had been asleep since the afternoon of the day before!

I felt groggy and stiff, like I needed to stretch. But when I tried to move, I couldn't! The right side of my back throbbed with pain, and I could hardly move my right arm or leg. The rest of my body felt numb and lifeless.

*My God! I'm paralyzed!*

Panic gripped me.

"Help!" I croaked, hoping someone would hear my feeble cry.

Moments later the skipper rushed in.

"I—I can't move!" I told him.

He just looked at me for a moment, then turned toward the door and called, "Angelo."

Almost immediately, Angelo—the corpsman—arrived, and together they examined me.

Looking at my injured face must have been enough to make most of the men feel a little queezy. I thought I looked bad enough *before* getting shot down. The *Bunker Hill* had crossed the equator only five days earlier, and during the shellback initiation, the Royal Barber, wielding his scissors with a vengeance, had gone after my hair, cropping it so unevenly I looked like a mole.

Added to that was the physical punishment I took hitting the plane's tail, getting pickled in salt water, grated over coral reefs and exposed to searing sun for several hours. I was a gruesome sight—hands and face blistered and shredded like hamburger; horrible purple bruises on my right arm and right leg, and a big, ugly welt across the right side of my back.

My face was such a mess at first that the crew nick-named me "prune face" after the Dick Tracy comic strip character.

I was a hideous sight when Sam Dealey and Angelo examined me. Dealey thought that I was probably just stiff from the long swim and the bad bruises on my arm and back. Maybe he was being a politician, because he knew that without a doctor on board there wasn't much they could do for me anyway...except stall for time to see.

Dealey then left, and Angelo continued examining me. He gently moved and twisted my arms and legs and found no broken bones. I had passed some blood and Angelo said it was from a damaged kidney—probably from getting wacked by the tail of my plane. I prayed that it wasn't ruptured.

Navy fighter pilots have reputations as effervescent guys with lots of ego and self-confidence. Right up until the time

160

I was shot down, that was exactly the image I projected.

But as I sat there in the exec's room on that submarine, I was a pathetic example of a guy who had really blown it. I knew it. The crew of the *Harder* knew it. And the whole Fifth Fleet knew it. I felt lower than a snake's belly.

Maybe those recruiters back in Chicago were right. Maybe I wasn't Naval Aviator material. Look at what I had done! I broke the rules by leaving formation, got myself shot down, wasted a brand new Hellcat, and the Navy had to send in air cover and a submarine to get me off an island. Can you imagine the dollar cost of all that? If they had docked my salary, I'd *still* be paying off the bill.

And believe me, I didn't look forward to facing my squadron commander. Boy! Was Collins ever going to be mad! I just wanted to crawl into a hole.


Even after all I had been through, there was still another humiliating incident. It centers on a personal and delicate topic which normally is not discussed in polite company, and I apologetically relate it here, doing so only to illustrate how far I had descended into the depths of humiliation.

Let me go back to when I was shot down and parachuted into the ocean. I was in the water for nearly five hours and must have gulped down half the Pacific. Well that salt water had a severe, uncontrollable laxative effect on my system. I had only been on board the sub for twenty or thirty minutes when nature called again, and I had to find the nearest bathroom—*fast*!

No big deal, right?

Wrong! Because I was on a *submarine*. And that makes a *big* difference.

Now, the bathroom on a ship is called a *head*, and, as I discovered, the toilet on a sub is a very sophisticated piece of plumbing—so much so that to use it requires special indoctrination on the complicated matter of operating its various valves and air and water lines. It took an engineer—or at least a very bright plumber—to figure it out.

I was neither. And believe me, right then, I was neither in the physical condition nor did I have the presence of mind (or the luxury of time) to take a Navy training course. But let me tell you that using that stainless steel contraption— that plumber's nightmare, that nemesis to a man in a hurry— turned out to be one of the most humiliating things ever to happen to me!

Because of my weakened condition and partial paralysis, two sailors helped me back to the nearest head. They immediately sensed the urgency of my dilemma and quickly scurried me down the narrow, light-gray passageway, en-route attempting enroute to give me a crash course in toilet-training *a la* submarine style. They told me I would find a lot of dials and some foot pedals, and to *carefully read* the instructions.

We arrived just in the nick of time. The head was next to the crews' quarters, and our arrival attracted the attention of a handful of off-duty sailors who lounged on their bunks amid the spare torpedoes that were lashed against the sides of the bulkheads.

"Be sure you follow the instructions," reminded one of the sailors, as they shoved me into the head and slammed the door, closing it with a bang.

The head was little more than a cubbyhole that appeared to be built into the sub as an afterthought. It was a confusing array of gauges, dials, valves and foot pedals. That place had more pipes and fittings than a hardware store. It must have been invented by Rube Goldberg.

*All this, just to go to the bathroom*? I thought. But I didn't have time to contemplate the scenery.

There I sat in that dimly lit, cramped little head, so tired and so sick. Because of what I had been through my vision was a little blurry anyway, but I tried my best to read how to use the toilet. The instructions said something about how you open this and close that, bleed in a little water, do your business, then close this and shut off that. There were two chambers—upper and lower. After using the upper chamber, its lid had to be clamped shut, and through various valves and pedals air pressure was used to transfer the contents into a lower chamber. This chamber then had to be charged with greater air pressure than the outside pressure of the sea so the contents could be expelled.

Well, it required reading pressure gauges. Dial *a* had to read greater than dial *b*, do steps *c* and *d*, don't do *x* and *y*.... As I said, it was very complicated, and I wasn't thinking too clearly.

By this time the sub was down to almost 300 feet where the pressure of the sea water was tremendous—all the more reason to properly read the gauges and operate the valves.

As you probably already know, yes, I got confused, misread gauges and pushed...the *wrong* pedal! There was a terrific explosion that blew me a foot off the toilet, and I crashed back down on the seat with a jolt.

Shell shock!

Everything in that chamber had been atomized and sprayed throughout the head. It was in my hair and my eyes, and it covered the bulkheads, the ceiling and all the plumbing. It left a mist in the air I will not offend you by describing.

There I sat dumbstruck with shock, to put it mildly. I heard the shuffle of feet outside the door, and several sailors yelling and laughing hilariously. They knew from the sound of the explosion what had happened. I was mortified! All I could do was sit there, feeling totally dejected, hurt and tired.

*What should I do?* I wondered.

"Zoomie, are you still there?" I heard the familiar voice of Keith Phillips.

"Yeah," I whispered in anguish, wishing I could have been anywhere else on earth at that moment. Oh, was I miserable!

"Come on out," urged Phillips, "we'll forgive you and clean it up this time."

I heard sniggering and guffaws from the others, and I cringed with humiliation.

*If only they'd just go away and leave me alone in my misery!*
But they didn't go away.

Phillips kept coaxing me: "The shower is right around to the left, Zoomie. Come out as you are."

I just sat there for another ten minutes. Finally, when I thought most of the men had returned to their stations, and I had mustered up enough nerve, I opened the door. Unfortunately I was next to the crews' quarters, and there were several sailors mingling around, not wanting to miss the fun when I came out.

There I stood, an unbelievable mess, naked except for my shorts, which were down around my ankles.

The sailors just about died laughing. All I could do was stand there idiotlike and take it. For obvious reasons, no one wanted to touch me, so, by myself, tail between my legs, I staggered over to the shower. I scrubbed and scrubbed and thought I could never get clean again.

Ensign Sampson insisted that I use his bunk for the rest of the cruise, which left him with only an army cot. Because of my injuries, it was a luxury I was grateful to have. I hit the sack and immediately conked out.

The next day, after awakening from another lengthy sleep, I was given some loaner clothes—a T-shirt, pants and shoes (but no socks). The shoes were two sizes too long and two sizes too narrow, but I managed to get into them. The pants legs stopped short—just above my ankles, and the shirt was skin-tight. I've seen better clothes in a thrift store.

Most of the men dressed only in sandals and shorts, with an optional T-shirt, and no socks. This was the uniform of the day, except for added clothing when going topside for watch. They dressed this way for a couple of very practical reasons. First, it was comfortable. Second, this type of lightweight, loosely-fitted clothing aided in the evaporation of body perspiration, which kept body odors down.

Don't think B.O. was simply a small social offense. The sub was air-conditioned, of course, but in times of attack, when it would dive and go to silent running, the air-conditioning equipment was turned off because the tell-tale sounds could be picked up by the enemy's sonar. With the air-conditioning off, the air became still, hot and humid—almost like a turkish bath—and then stale with odors. In the cramped quarters of a silent-running submarine, the air could turn bad enough by itself, but with excessive body odors, it turned foul enough to make you cough...or worse.

There were eleven officers on board, including myself, and since the officers' wardroom accommodated only six, we were divided into two shifts for meals. Sam Dealey invited me to dine with him in the first shift, and I think he wanted to cheer me up because my spirits were down. And, boy, did I need cheering up!

This was my third day on the sub, and only now was I feeling well enough to eat a meal. I couldn't use my right arm to eat, so I temporarily had to learn how to be a southpaw. Then I remembered my last meal—aboard the *Bunker Hill*, with the chaplain sitting across from me. What was it he had said?—"You might not eat again today!" How prophetic! I didn't eat again that day or the next.

A fighter pilot without his plane is almost useless! Like a cowboy without his horse. And an aviator on a submarine is totally out of his environment. A real bird in the water. I didn't even have my snappy Naval Aviator's khaki uniform to strut around in! I felt like a creature from outer space (and even looked like something from another world!).

For the first few days I was a curiosity. The men of the *Harder* questioned me about airplanes and what it was like to be a fighter pilot. I was too embarrased to talk much about it right then, because my ego was deflated for ignoring the cardinal rule in fighter tactics, which is why I got shot down. So I did my best to turn the conversation away from myself and in the direction of the men and their submarine.

Navy protocol never seemed to hinder my relationship with Sam Dealey. Though many of our conversations were casual and personal in nature, Sam displayed a leadership quality that made me admire and respect him. Not all our conversations were on personal matters; he was only too pleased to talk about the submarine Navy, and as I came to know him better, I discovered he had a very real love affair going with the *Harder*.

I learned from Sam that the sub had just come on station from Pearl Harbor and was now on its fourth patrol. "If we survive," he winked, "we're going to Australia."

"*If?*" I asked myself. I gulped and said nothing, secretly wondering if he was serious or just had a twisted sense of humor. I wasn't particularly fond of water *before* my ordeal in the ocean, and I wasn't too keen about having to persevere for long on this submerged, overgrown thermos bottle.

Then Sam let me in for a real blow: by now, the *Bunker Hill*, along with the rest of the fleet, had moved miles out of the area, leaving the *Harder* behind. The sub was on a secret mission, and its orders would not permit it to return me to a carrier.

"We'll be out here for thirty days, Zoomie," Sam told me with a smile, "maybe sixty days. It looks like you're in for some submarine duty before we can drop you off in Australia."

*Sixty days!* I thought. *In this floating sardine can?*

Then, for the first time, I thought about rejoining my squadron—something I did not look forward to. I knew that Collins, my CO, was really going to be upset with me for getting shot down and being away from the squadron for so long.

As long as I was stuck on the sub, I might as well make the best of it.

Sam Dealey included me in everything. He did his best to make me feel welcome and constantly pumped me up after my ordeal. He liked having me join him for meals in the officers' wardroom. His seat was at the end of the table and mine was to his right.

One of our favorite topics was to analyze what had happened when I bailed out of my plane. We looked at all the elements—my injuries, the torn life jacket, the torn rubber boat and the rip cord still in the pocket. We pieced it together this way: when my body left the plane and entered the blast of wind, it must have rotated so the tail gave me a terrific slap—hitting me along the right side and tearing into the bulky, protruding seat pack, ripping the boat and life jacket, and slashing the flaps of the parachute container. This released the spring-loaded pilot chute, which snapped out, pulling the main canopy into the windblast where it instantly popped open. I was probably a low 300 feet off the surface of the water, but because of the high speed, my body arched in a horizontal trajectory that allowed enought time for the chute to open. One swing and I hit the drink.

Sam and I agreed that had I missed the tail, there would not have been sufficient time for me to manually pull the D-ring and the chute to open fully.

Talk about a miracle!

As I write this incredible story nearly four decades after it took place, do you notice one obvious ommission? What about all those "The Lord is My Shepherds?" What about all those cries for help in the water? There is not a single word about my giving thanks and praising God for my deliverance from the sea. I'll tell you why: because I didn't even think to thank God. I could pray loud and clear when I was afraid and needed help, but it was so easy to forget God after He provided for my rescue.

And this is true today in so many peoples' lives. When we have a problem we cannot solve, or find ourselves in a box canyon of difficulties, we pray for help and guidance. Then when the Lord does intervene, and the problem is solved or cleared up, we forget to give thanks, or we accept the conclusion as something *we* did ourselves, and say things like, "Boy, that was *fortunate!*" Or, "Wasn't I *lucky!*"

# 14
# Sam's Tactics

Sam Dealey's warm personality became more apparent as I got to know him better. He had a gentleness about him—a tender way of ministering to my wounded ego, and a slow, easy smile that let me know he understood the dejection and humiliation I felt. I needed a friend right then, and in meeting that need, Sam came to my rescue a second time.

I guess my low self-esteem caused me to imagine that I was going to be scorned by the *Harder's* crew, but instead I was accepted immediately and began making friends with the officers and enlisted men.

That's important in a sub. It's a small world to live in, and one loner or rotten egg can mess up morale and even jeopardize the mission and safety of a sub and its crew. If someone doesn't fit in, then out he goes.

This actually happened to one of the men. He didn't fit in as a team-member and was later transferred out and assigned to shore duty.

Well, I did my best to fit in.

Within the span of a few days, I was hobbling around the *Harder* under my own steam, exploring every nook and cranny. Evidently my kidney had only been bruised and was now healed. Feeling and strength were returning to my right arm and leg. At first I got stabbing pains whenever I went through the small, water-tight doors that separated the compartments. Because of this, I kept pretty much to one small area of the sub. But after a few days, the pain gradually went away.

Most of all, I was getting over my injured pride and Sam Dealey was largely responsible for helping me do that.

To begin with, I had to get some things straight with myself as well as in my relationship with the crew. I needed to overcome my humiliation and regain some self-respect, plus I owed those men a debt of gratitude for their trouble and risks in rescuing me. The last thing I wanted to do was sit around and do nothing—to be a gold-brick. I figured as long as I was going to be aboard, I might as well make the best of it. And I'll have to admit I still had a little pride left, because I was determined to convince those salty submariners that a zoomie was as adept underwater as in the air.

What kind of work can a displaced zoomie do on a submarine? I did some private investigating. Obviously I knew nothing about navigation at sea, so that was out, and after my sorry solo in the head I knew the engine room wasn't a place for me. Finally I ran across a couple of jobs I felt comfortable with. As soon as I was physically able to work, I asked Sam to let me assume the total responsibility of encoding and decoding messages sent and received by the sub, and also to stand watch along with the rest of the officers and crew. He was more than happy to oblige.

I liked the coding job because it gave me the chance to know about everything that was being communicated between the *Harder* and Pearl Harbor. It wasn't a job that took a lot of knowledge—I simply used a code book to translate outgoing messages into crypt and reversed the process with incoming messages. I didn't have to know how to use the radio; there was an enlisted man to handle that end of the job. Choice duty!

The Navy required this kind of two-man operation for security reasons. I didn't know how to use the radio and the radio man didn't have a code book. This was a workable check in the event a saboteur infiltrated the sub's ranks.

At first, I thought that standing watch would be boring and monotonous. But after several stints I found I enjoyed it. In rough water I liked to stand on the bridge, brace myself with both hands and watch the bow cut through the waves. I felt like I was the master of the sea!

I should explain that the conning tower lookout consisted of the officer-of-the-deck and after deck and four enlisted men who kept their eyes glued to binoculars, scanning the sea and skies for enemy ships and planes. Our duty schedule was four hours on the bridge, then four hours off.

I was actually beginning to enjoy my new tour of duty. It helped pass the time, and besides, I felt I was making a real contribution.

It wasn't long until the other officers remarked to Sam what a welcome relief it was to have me take over the coding duties. Someone even jokingly suggested that Sam rescue a downed zoomie on every trip!

Little did I know back on that morning of April 1, when I flew off the deck of the *Bunker Hill*, that I would temporarily become a submarine officer!

For several days following my rescue, the *Harder* had the sea to herself. We encountered no enemy ships or planes, and life on board settled down to routine watches, drills and training.

I learned that subs ran on the surface all the time—except when making a torpedo run on an enemy ship or eluding attacking Jap destroyers or planes. When running submerged, the diesel engines were quieted and battery-driven electric motors used. Maximum surface speed was twenty-one knots, while only nine knots maximum could be achieved submerged—which quickly drained the batteries.

There were similarities between fighter tactics and sub tactics. For example, a pilot's best defense was to escape from the enemy by hiding in the clouds or running away in a steep dive. It was much the same for a sub: dive down deep to elude depth charges dropped by planes or destroyers.

Once a sub is under attack, it can waste no time in diving. For this reason diving drills were held regularly, the objective being to reduce the time required. Hearing Sam's command to dive, each man knew his duties like second-nature, and never had to ask himself, "Now, what do I do next?" The crew became so proficient that we could go from surface to a depth of 100 feet in fifty-five seconds.

When I wasn't on watch or in the radio shack, I usually roamed about, talking with the crew and investigating their incredibly efficient underwater war machine. All the officers thought zoomies were crazy to fly an airplane when they could be in a sub—this was the *real* weapon!

Not only was the *Harder* a weapon, it was home—a totally self-contained community. I was amazed at how its crew of eighty-four could live and work in such close quarters. Everything we needed was there, ingeniously fitted into place, with every nook and cranny utilized for something. Even the Momsen escape hatchway was stuffed full of gunny sacks of potatoes and onions! Not a square inch of space was squandered.

The sub was actually larger than I had imagined. Although it was very narrow, it was as long as a football field and within its hull (doubled throughout, except for the fore and aft torpedo rooms) were housed enormous fuel tanks, ballast tanks, batteries, engine rooms, ammunition rooms and the control rooms, plus, of course, the crew's galley, officers' wardroom and sleeping areas.

The control room, the nerve center of the boat, was immediately below the conning tower. Sam stationed himself here to command the sub. What a job! Sam carried an incredible amount of responsibility. Not only did he command the operation of the sub, but he also manned the periscope and personally directed attacks. Nearby were the sonar and radar operators who kept in direct contact with him whenever the sub was pursuing a fat Jap freighter or being hunted down by a Nip plane or a depth-charge laden destroyer.

On the deck beside the control room was the navigation compartment, where the plotting table was located.

Sam and Frank Lynch, the executive officer, were constantly bending over the plotting board, studying the map and charting our course. Frank did the navigating and his quips were returned with constant teasing by Sam on his method of computing position.

One day Sam asked him where we were, and Frank said quite nonchalantly, "Damn if I know, Captain!" It took me a few seconds to catch on that Frank wasn't serious.

When Sam and Frank went off duty they were relieved by the second-string headed by Sam Logan and Tom Buckner as chief engineer and diving officer, with Finney or Levin working at the Torpedo Data Center. This was part of Sam's program to have back-up officers who would know the procedure of approach and attack.

One day as I walked past Sam's compartment I noticed he was reading the Bible. I didn't disturb him, but continued on my way with greater admiration for him because he was a religious man.

I came to know Sam as a pleasant, easy-going friend, who was quick to smile and slow to anger. But underneath that laid-back demeanor was a man with a burning desire to achieve perfection in his duties as a submarine commander. He wanted to do his job to the utmost—and more.

At that time and stage of the war, submarine tactics were limited to lifeguarding and sinking slow-moving cargo- and fuel-laden freighters, and occasionally warships, if they got in the way. But Sam had the aggressive mind of a hunter, and his fertile imagination was always contemplating innovative ways to go after other kinds of Jap sea-going targets. Sam was also driven by a personal score he had to settle; his roommate at the Naval Academy, Tex Edwards, had been lost when the Germans sank the destroyer *Reuben James*, the first ship lost by America in World War II.

"Zoomie, come into the wardroom; I want to talk to you for a few minutes." I followed Sam Dealey into the *Harder's* cramped but functional officers' dining room, and we sat down across the table from each other.

"I've got a theory, and I want to bat it around with you." A gleam of excitement danced in the Captain's gold-flecked brown eyes, as he continued in his slow Texas drawl: "Zoomie, let's assume you're a bright, young Jap commander who graduated out of the Saki Academy, and you're the skipper of one of Nippon's nice new destroyers. You're out on patrol and one of your lookouts screams, 'periscope!' What would you do?"

I hesitated. Being a fighter pilot, I knew little about a submarine's operation or what a Jap destroyer skipper would do. "Well, Captain Dealey," I answered slowly, a little unsure of myself, "I'd probably order all ahead full, sound general quarters, and turn toward that periscope."

His thin, black mustache curled into a slight grin—of approval, yes, but more than that, as if he knew something I didn't know.

"And what do you think that sub is going to do?" he asked.

"Why, turn and run, I guess—or dive deep to escape the depth-charges."

"You're right! That's what subs are *supposed* to do!"

The way he stressed *supposed* made me wary.

"I didn't know zoomies were that intelligent!" he said with a wry grin.

175

It was a good-natured rub, not at all disparaging.

After allowing himself the little joke at my expense, the skipper returned to the scenario of the submarine and the destroyer.

"This time the confrontation is different. You're steaming toward the *'melican pig boat's* periscope, but strangely, the sub doesn't turn and run. Instead, one of your lookouts screams: 'Torpedo!' And sure enough, you see the frothy wake of a torpedo knifing through the water straight for your bow. What would you do?"

"Why, order 'turn,' of course," I said, thinking that even a zoomie is *that* intelligent!

"Precisely! Precisely!" he exclaimed, almost jumping out of his chair. "So would I!"

I smiled sheepishly with relief at gaining his approval, but still felt uncertain about what he was leading up to. And what he said next was so astonishing and preposterous it made my scalp crawl!

"My plan," he said, "is to deliberately attack destoyers and sink them."

My mouth dropped wide open. *This guy is nuts!* I thought. But Sam kept on talking.

"You see, Zoomie, when that destroyer skipper sees my torpedo coming straight at him, he *must* turn one way or the other, and I plan to have a couple of torpedoes waiting for him whichever direction he goes!

"After all, Zoomie, what is a destroyer? It's a thin-hulled ship, highly maneuverable at high speeds, with the capability of sinking submarines. And, other than a light cruiser or another submarine, they're the only ones that can defend themselves against a marauding submarine or a pack of submarines.

"We've known for a long time that the Japanese fleet is desperately short of destoyers. So rather than keeping carriers, battleships and cruisers as target priorities, we should be hunting down destroyers and tankers. Then, the whole Japanese navy would be defenseless against our ships, planes and submarines. I aim to prove that a submarine can successfully attack a destroyer—by plan, not just chance—and I'm trying to promote the idea that we should change our priorities in the submarine navy.''

I felt a little queezy. He was *serious*! He had the whole thing backwards. He was David taking on Goliath! The minnow going after the big fish! The fox chasing the hound! He was plumb crazy! I was safer *before* he rescued me—back on that island, taking my chances against the Japs! *Out of the frying pan and into the fire!*

As it turned out, the sages at Pearl Harbor would have none of Sam's "foolishness"—not at first, anyway. But this brilliant young sub skipper's status was growing in their eyes. Hadn't he just pulled off a fantastic rescue that the whole fleet was buzzing about? For now, Admiral Charles A. Lockwood, Commander, Submarines, Pacific Fleet, put a ban on Sam's wishes to go destroyer-hunting, citing that it would waste torpedoes and unjustifiably jeopardize the lives of crewmen.

*Good for "Charlie" Lockwood!*

# 15

## Sam Baits a Destroyer

Sam told me I would be stuck on the *Harder* for one to two months while it put in lifeguard duty around Woleai Atoll. The place was an insignificant little string of coral islands, located halfway between Truk and New Guinea, with an airfield the Japs used as a staging area and refueling stop for airplanes. That's why Admiral Spruance of the Fifth Fleet ordered us carrier pilots to give it a plastering. And that's when I got shot down, only to be rescued by the *Harder*.

But now things had quieted down to uneventful lifeguard duty. There was no American action in our area, and time dragged on. The only excitement was the spasmodic appearance of Jap patrol planes.

The damage we aviators had inflicted on Woleai seemed to have been repaired at this point because anti-submarine aircraft coverage over the area appeared to be heavier and more consistent than ever. Everytime a Jap plane flew near us, Sam routinely took the sub down until danger passed. It happened again and again. ("This is getting monotonous," he noted in the sub's log.)

I learned that submariners have a natural distrust of airplanes—even our own! More than once an American flyer had bombed one of our subs, mistaking it for a Japanese boat.

Everyone looked forward to the end of the Woleai patrol when the *Harder* would be transferred from COMSUBPAC in Pearl to COMSUBSOWESPAC in Freemantle, Australia, and from there, hopefully, back into the heat of combat.

The *Harder's* crew thrived on combat, and now that they were removed from action, boredom became the number one enemy. You did whatever you could to keep occupied and pass the time. On a sub, I soon discovered, there aren't many options. After you've read everything there is to read and caught up on letter-writing, there isn't much left to do.

The juke box was a novelty for a while. Frank Lynch had miraculously come across it at Pearl. It was the kind with brilliant, luminous red, yellow, blue and green liquid bubbling through glass tubes. What a sensation! It was constantly blasting out popular songs as off-duty men gathered around it, keeping time by tapping toes and snapping fingers. Now it was seldom played. We tired of hearing the familiar songs over and over. At first, the songs reminded us of fond memories of home, but then they became painful reminders that life on the *Harder* had become stagnant and void of anything new.

Because of the inactivity, the crew became as edgy as caged tigers, and Sam taxed his mind to come up with something to break the monotony.

The doldrum days were just as wearing on the officers. Down in the wardroom, the sub boys spun tall stories about how they do it in the "Silent Service," while old Galvin, with no one around to disclaim him, told how the zoomies do it in the air and what it's like to fly a fighter plane.

Then, unexpectedly, the humdrum routine was finally broken the night of April 12-13. I was on decoding duty in

180

the radio shack when the message came in that Sam had been hoping and praying for: "Lollipalooser for the *Harder*...Target priority restrictions lifted." Sam could now go after Jap destroyers!

Several days later the periscope watch spotted the mast of a Jap destroyer resting in Woleai's lagoon. Apparently it had come in the previous night, under the cover of darkness.

Sam was elated over the discovery—and eager to put his plan into motion.

"We're going to travel on the surface every minute of the day," he announced to the crew, "and when you spot a Jap plane, I want you to sing it out. But the officer in charge of the bridge is *not* to sound the diving alarm until the Jap plane definitely commits himself toward our location, thereby acknowledging that he has seen the sub."

Afterwards the *Harder* was indeed spotted by a few Jap patrol planes. This prompted Sam to call all of us officers to the wardroom. "What's been going on," he began to explain, "is we've been baiting that little Nip in the harbor. Now, you may think this is crazy, but I've been staying on the surface until several Jap patrol planes spotted us. If we show ourselves enough times, somebody on that destroyer is going to get nervous and come out looking for us. We're going to be bait— for a trap. And we're going to sink that destroyer."

Well, that just tied my guts in knots! *Holy Mackerel*, I thought, *We're in the company of a maniac!*

While the news was also a shock to some of the other officers, they felt "If Sam Dealey says that's what we're going to do, then that's what we're going to do!" What confidence in their skipper! And why not? They'd had three highly successful combat patrols with him. I'd have to learn to trust him too.

For three days we baited the airplanes to sight us, commit to us, then down we'd dive. Sam had fine-honed the crew to where, from the time he punched the diving horn, they could have the sub down to 100 feet in fifty-five seconds. When the tip of the periscope dipped beneath, Sam ordered, "Hard right rudder," or "hard left rudder." Moments later bombs dropped on our foamy track, but never really close. The Japs didn't know how deep and quickly we could dive, consequently they set depth charges to explode at depths too shallow. I just hoped a plane wouldn't misplace dropping a bomb and sink us by accident!

The frying pan was getting hotter.

The *Harder* was cruising on the surface, with Sam in his customary place on the bridge. He never let me go topside during the day, only at night, because he always wanted his more experienced men up there during the day when we were more vulnerable to attack. If anything was going on, I was generally in the main control room, which was just below the conning tower control room. During those times I just nosed around and observed what the crew was doing.

The periscope could be used from either the main control room or up in the conning tower.

The conning tower control room contained the quartermaster's wheel, periscope, Torpedo Data Computer, and the Dead Reckoning Tracking Table. Here is where the submerged action took place.

The main control room contained the same elements as the conning tower control room plus all other functions for running the sub—depth gauge, bow and stern plane controls, radar, etc. During depth charging, everyone came down out of the upper room, since the conning tower was not double hulled.

This day, April 14, was typically hot and boring. It was a typical day for Carl Finney, too, but typical to him meant it was a day of potential hazard. He was the well-disciplined warrant officer in charge who gave his full attention to watching the circular sweep of the white line on the radar scope, and was quick to respond to the tell-tale blip of an approaching aircraft or surfaceship.

At 1446 the routine silence of the control room was broken when Carl yelled out: "There's another plane, Cap'n. Bearing zero-two-zero, relative...distance, four miles."[1]

Sam scanned the horizon through binoculars until he located the plane. He watched as it banked and turned in the direction of the *Harder*.

"Clear the bridge!" he ordered the five other men topside. "Dive, dive...." he shouted into the boat's telephone to the control room.

In automatic response to the captain's order, someone below hit the klaxon switch and it squawked its *awgoowa* alarm throughout the sub. As the periscope slid down, Sam watched the conning tower hatch while one-by-one the lookouts and bridge watch disappeared down the ladder into the bowels of the boat. Sam gave a final glance about the bridge to be sure all hands were below. Then he rushed over to the hatch and slid down the ladder, as the *Harder's* nose slid beneath the surface and white foam washed over her foreward deck.

As soon as Sam dropped through the hatch he barked out: "Give her hard right rudder. All ahead full. Take her to 100 feet."

The next few minutes would tell if he was successful in ditching the plane.

With *Harder's* nose angled downward and the dive well underway, Sam called out to Frank Lynch and the other men in the attack control group, myself included, to follow him down to the wardroom for "a little council of war."

We gathered around what served as our dining room table watching Sam, waiting for him to speak, and studying the sparkle of excitement in his eyes. I knew what that look meant, and it scared me stiff!

Sam reviewed his plan with us, and when there were no more questions he asked Ray Levin to hand him the public address microphone. He was ready to reveal the plan to all on board. Pausing before speaking into the microphone, he looked around the circle of officers and smiled. Then, in his soft but authoritative voice, he spoke.

"We've been on a little fishing expedition this afternoon," Sam's voice sounded over the squawk box throughout the sub. The men stared at the speakers, as if to understand their Skipper more clearly.

"*Harder* was the hook and the bait, and the fish we were after was an airplane pilot who would sight us and radio back to his base for a destroyer to come and give us a dose of ashcans. There just aren't any worthwhile targets around here, so I aim to catch us a Jap tincan."

*Crazy! Just plain crazy!* I thought, nervously scanning the faces of the other officers. No one said a word, but I guessed they were all thinking the same thoughts: it was a crazy idea and a dangerous one. But if Sam said it was a plan that would work, then it was a deal.

"Some of you may think that destroyers are dangerous game and more deadly to subs than we are to them," he continued. "Don't you believe it. An American sub can put a Nip DD down for the count any day....And if you all don't believe me, I sure hope I'll have a chance to prove it."[2]

It wouldn't be honest to say there wasn't apprehension written on the faces of several men. For most of them, it was the first time they had heard of their skipper's daring tactic. But like the ship's officers, they, too, had confidence in him.

The more I thought about it, the more I was beginning to think Sam Dealey's plan just might work. I was beginning to realize that he was no ordinary sub captain. He was a maverick genius whose thinking was far ahead of the Japanese Navy— and our own Navy as well!

Every fifteen minutes the sub rose to periscope depth and Sam, gritting his pipe between his teeth and peering through the eyepiece of the periscope, would scan the skies in search of a Jap patrol plane.

Each time Sam did this, I held my breath and wondered, *Is this it? Is this when we stick our heads in the lion's mouth?*

Time and again Sam scanned the horizon and the sky, only to see endless miles of empty ocean.

No ships.

No planes.

Sam continued patiently until, that afternoon, one of the boys on the sonar reported that he heard pinging. A quick check of SJ radar showed there were no planes. Right away a very excited skipper flew up to the conning tower, and up went the periscope. He knew there was only one kind of ship that pinged—a destroyer. He could hardly believe it was true! He told the quartermaster to head the sub on a direct course toward the location of the suspected destroyer.

The pinging indicated the destroyer's sonar was on a swinging, circular sweep, scanning the depths for a submarine in a full, 360-degree circle. We would hear pinging come into audible range, fade out, and then come back into range. No doubt the destroyer's radar was on a circular sweep, too.

As the *Harder* came around to starboard, aiming its bow toward the distant destroyer, our sonar's pinging became louder.

Minutes later the sonarman reported the rotational sound had stopped, and that now the target was doing a sector search, narrowing down its sonar sweep to fifteen to twenty degrees. That could only mean the destroyer had us pin-pointed on its sonar and was coming in for the bait! That Jap skipper must have been feeling sure he was about to sink an American sub!

At 1610, while Sam was searching the broad expanse of ocean through the periscope, his keen eyes spotted a dark speck—a plane—just above the horizon. He kept his eyes on it as it grew larger and larger. Moments later, after comparing the image with silhouettes in the ONI book, he identified it as a land-based medium Jap bomber.

The plane circled the area in broad sweeps, coming within two miles of where the *Harder* lay submerged. Then, surprisingly, the plane turned north and headed out of sight. Had the pilot seen the sub's silhouette?

Five minutes later that question was answered. Sam sighted the faint lines of a destroyer's mast, not more than six miles away.

For some unknown reason the plane never came back. If it had, Sam would have abandoned his plan and ordered the sob to dive to escape tha plane's dapth charge. But there was no plane in sight!

The Jap destroyer was steaming directly toward us. Sam, displaying nerves of steel, kept the *Harder* on a steady course, straight toward the approaching killer. We were committed now, and there was no turning back. It was either the destroyer or us! My heart began to pound, and as I looked around at the rest of the crew, I sensed the mounting tension.

I wondered what it was like aboard that Jap destroyer. No doubt the tension was getting to them, too, because they saw our periscope bob up to the surface periodically. In that Jap skipper's mind, we had to be either a Jap sub that had not identified itself, or we were an American sub that had not seen them.

Regardless, the destroyer continued to bear down on us at full speed. We were playing a deadly game of cat and mouse, only this time the mouse would not turn and run.

186

# 16

# Going for the Kill

"**B**attle Stations!" bellowed Sam Dealey over the *Harder's* public address system. The excitement in his voice told us this was the moment the skipper had been waiting for. Jittery nerves tensed our muscles as tight as wound-up mainsprings, so when we moved, we literally sprang into action. I flew in to the main control room and stood shaking in my sandals, my heart going thumpety-thump in triple time.

The attack team hurriedly assembled on the deck above me in the conning tower. I could envision them taking up their positions while Sam, with his eyes glued to the periscope, anxiously watched and waited for the Jap destroyer to sail into view.

Moments later sonar reported the Jap destroyer was coming straight for us...then radar chimed in to confirm the report.

Frank Lynch, with the responsibilities of assistant attack officer added to his duties as exec, stood right at the skipper's side, relaying Sam's special orders to the crew. Occasionally, on his own initiative, Frank gave orders for routine procedures, in order to allow Sam full concentration on the target and the attack strategy.

Sam Logan was at Torpedo Data Control. Number one in the Class of '42 at the Naval Academy, he was a brilliant thinker, and many times had a correct answer as fast as the computer. Keith Phillips and Phil Sampson hovered over the plotting table figuring the position of the destroyer in relation to the sub.

Some sub skippers liked to turn the periscope over to their assistant attack officer, in order to keep their mind free when the time arrived to move in for the kill, but not Sam Dealey; he was always on the periscope during General Quarters. The way he saw it, when a sub is running underwater, there is only one person who can see what is going on, and on the *Harder* he was that man. Besides, this new destroyer-killing strategy was his brainchild, and he was not about to let anyone else run the show.

As the destroyer came closer, Sam crisply called out its description and markings. Lynch thumbed through the ONI book, looking for a matching silhouette. He located it and held the book up for the skipper to see. Sam was pleased to discover that the ship was not one of the older tincans that normally were used for minor escort duties, but one of the brand-new, 1950-ton destroyers of the *Fubuki* class (later identified as the *Ikazuchi*).

"One-third speed ahead," Sam ordered.

"One-third speed ahead," Frank acknowledged, relaying the order.

Periodically, Sam corrected the course to keep the sub's nose pointed directly at the destroyer, giving the tincan's sonar the smallest possible target. Curiously, the sky was clear of any Jap planes that might spot the silhouette of our submerged sub and report its exact location to the tincan.

As the day drew to a close and the sun sank below the horizon, there was less risk of the sub's being sighted by the destroyer's lookouts. Now Sam was ready to move the *Harder* in closer to set up the attack.

My thoughts turned to the incredible chain of circumstances that brought me to this time and place. There I was, Ensign John R. Galvin, fighter pilot, standing at the foot of the ladder in the main control room of a submarine watching Sam Dealey as he began to write a new chapter in the annals of submarine warfare.

My memory drew back to the role-playing Sam and I did, and to that imaginary Jap skipper, as his proud new "Nippon destroyer" plied the waters looking for our periscope.

I could just picture him—that graduate of "Saki Academy"—standing on the bridge when he sees a torpedo coming straight for his ship! He'll have no choice but to turn out of its path. And that's exactly what Sam wants him to do!

The distance narrowed between the oncoming destroyer and the *Harder* and I could overhear Sam and the other members of the attack team as they tracked it.

Carl Finney was standing beside me when we started to hear the distance countdown. The distance was 5000 yards at 1847. From that point on, the radar man called out the range every 1000 yards.

"Make ready four tubes forward and four tubes aft!" I heard Sam order over the squawkbox. *Eight fish!* I thought. *Wow! How can he miss?* Now was his long awaited chance, and he wasn't about to lose this prize through misses or dud torpedoes.

"Four thousand yards and closing, Cap'n," we heard Wilbur Clark, the sonar operator report, sensing the intensity in his tone. Wilbur, from Hampton, Missouri, was on his first cruise aboard the *Harder*, and already had developed into a skilled sonar operator.

"Hey, Finney," I whispered through nervous, dry lips, "what's the normal range for shooting off the torpedoes?"

"Relax, Zoomie, the skipper knows what he's doing."

But I *couldn't* relax, and asked again, trying to be as nonchalant as possible: "Under normal conditions, what's the firing range?"

"Oh, about 2500 yards."

I could just picture in my mind two knife-edged ships racing at each other.

Yard by yard, we crept closer to the approaching destroyer. Except for the loud pounding of my heart, about the only other sound was the increasing loudness of the destroyer's pinging.

"Three thousand yards, Cap'n...."

We hardly needed to be told we were getting closer. The destroyer's more frequent pings were echoing through the sub's hull with a loud shrillness that was almost maddening in itself.

Moments later, almost in unison, the radarman and sonarman called out, "2500 yards, Cap'n!"

*Well, we're going to shoot now,* I thought. But Sam *didn't* shoot!

The Jap skipper was no fool. Wilbur reported the destroyer had started to zigzag on a course that would take it to within 800 to 1000 yards from us. *Will Sam's strategy still work against a zigzagging destroyer?* I wondered. *Oh, boy, this is hopeless!*

"Two thousand yards, Cap'n...."

Now we were close enough for Wilbur Clark to pick up a good turn count of the enemy's props. At 2600 yards, he reported: "About 135 to 140 rpms—fourteen to fifteen knots, Cap'n."

Until now, Sam had enjoyed good visibility. But at this crucial point the sun was setting almost directly behind the destroyer and its low rays were blinding. Sam quickly fitted the sun filter into place over the eye piece, and though it was a nuisance, it did help.

"Fifteen hundred yards, Cap'n...." And after that report, Wilbur reported every 100 yards.

At this point when the destroyer stopped zigzagging, and our sonar reported he was boring straight in on us. Wilbur

Clark reported an increase in the on-coming destroyer's turn-count, and Sam muttered that the ship's bow wave had increased. The destroyer was bearing down on us at full speed!

"Left full rudder," snapped Sam, his eyes fixed at the periscope, giving the order that would bring the *Harder* bow on bow with the charging destroyer. Sam ordered the gyro angle for the torpedoes in the bow tubes set at zero—he was getting so close that at the last second he would have to rely on his own aim to send the deadly missiles on the right trajectory.

"Eleven hundred yards, Cap'n...."

"Well," came Sam's calm, reassuring voice over the squawkbox, "This is where we're going to prove our theory. It's him or us! We're bow onto each other—he's coming full blast, and we're ready. We won't have much longer to wait."

"One thousand...."

*Oh, no!* I murmured.

"Nine hundred...."

Sam gave out a yelp that startled me so much I jumped. Then he started rattling off a string of fast orders.

"Oh, the dumb, stupid jerk," I heard him mutter about the Jap skipper, who was steaming right into the trap.

We were still bow on bow, the destroyer at full speed and the *Harder* at one-third. Then at the last instant, the destroyer made an abrupt turn. Evidentially, because we were so close, the Jap's sonar began sounding confusing pings and the sound man's interpretation was that we had turned!

But the destroyer's unexpected turn meant that Sam's firing plan had to be changed—and fast! Sam wasn't *about* to let the destroyer get away. "Right full rudder!" he ordered, then followed that by several more rapid orders. As the sub turned, we picked up lead and Sam called out, "Match gyros." Logan quickly keyed the command into the TDC and the computer automatically calculated a new gyro angle for the torpedoes.

Now Sam wouldn't have to fire the first torpedo point-blank to force the destroyer to turn—the Jap skipper turned voluntarily! All Sam had to do was give the destroyer a little lead and start firing!

Finally I heard what we'd all been waiting to hear: "Fire one!" yelled Sam. And at eight-second intervals: "Fire two!...Fire three!...Fire four!"

Sam was getting a good look at the destroyer as the torpedoes white-trailed their way to the target.

"Down scope!" he yelled. "Take her down...dive, dive!"

"Aye, aye, Cap'n," someone answered. And as the klaxon clanged loudly, the crew was already responding. I felt the sub's nose dip forward.

"Emergency hard right rudder...all ahead full."

*Emergency? Now what?*

The sub heeled over slightly, as it leaned into a sharp turn, and all I could imagine was that the destroyer was about to ram us. But that wasn't the problem at all; Sam just wanted to clear the area to escape the concussion of the explosions when the torpedoes hit their mark.

Someone with a stop-watch up in the conning tower control room was counting off the seconds until the torpedoes, moving at forty miles per hour, should reach their target.

"Five seconds...four...three...two...one...." Silence.

Nothing!

*Did he miss?*

And then...*balloomm!* We felt the concussion of a distant explosion. A cheer went up throughout the sub!

*Sam got the destroyer!*

*Balloomm!* There goes torpedo number two! And after that there was nothing to be heard on the sub but wild cheering.

Sam had hastily fired four torpedoes, all set with small gyro angles, which is the equivalent of a gunfighter shooting from the hip! Sam had hoped to score with at least one, but he had made direct hits with *two*!

*My God! He did it!* Sam had actually drawn that destroyer into a trap and torpedoed it!

I turned to Finney and said confidently, "I *knew* he would do it!"

There was shouting and cheering and laughing on the *Harder* like nothing I'd ever heard.

Sam ordered the sub up to periscope depth, and called for all the officers to come up and take a look. After the ship's officers took their turns, Sam called down to me and said: "Zoomie, this is the way we do it!" He gestured for me to take a look. I pressed my face against the eyepiece and peered through the scope. The stern end of the destroyer—probably a third of the ship's length—was sticking almost straight up out of the water. By now the *Harder* was only 400 yards from the sinking ship, and with the periscope snapped into its twenty-power lens, I could plainly see the Japs hanging onto the rails as she went down. I shared Sam's feeling of triumph over sinking the *Ikazuchi* and his hatred for all of Tojo's depth-charge-tossing destroyers, but the sight of that ship, slipping nose-first beneath the water, carrying its crew to their death, was something I could no longer watch.

Frank Lynch snapped a camera on the other periscope, and started taking pictures.

Just when I thought things had calmed down, Sam ordered, "Emergency! Clear the area." And we were rocked by explosion after explosion. I thought—and I think everybody else thought too—that we were being depth charged or had collided with the sinking destroyer. But Sam came on the squawkbox and put our minds at ease: "Don't worry, men, those are the depth charges that were stacked up on the destroyer's racks with their fuses all set for us, and they're going off at various depths as the destroyer sinks into the deep."

From the time the destroyer was hit, it took only four minutes for it to slip out of sight beneath the water's surface.

Sam ordered the *Harder* to dive and cleared the area at two-thirds speed, staying down in the event the tincan might have sent a distress signal to any other destroyers or planes in the area.

Then Sam and the rest of us could relax and savor the taste of triumph over sinking the destroyer. As apprehensive as I had been, I didn't panic. This had happened to other men on other subs, jeopardizing the safety of the crew and the boat. I learned later that control room chiefs were instructed to cold-cock anyone who panicked. Maybe that's why Finney stuck so close to me.

Sam turned to his exec and said, "You see, Frank, they really aren't invulnerable. They won't float with a couple of holes in their bottoms.... Well, there's one for the old *Reuben James*—and a down-payment for some of the bad times they gave us off Honshu."[1]

Hours later, when Sam was catching up on his log entries, he penned a colorful, though simple and modest account of the attack which changed the history of American submarine warfare. Here, in his own words, is how the attack was carried out:

"1859—Range now 900 yards. Commenced firing. Expended four torpedoes and one Jap destroyer! The four bow shots were fired at mean range of 900 yards, with a two-degree diverging spread, track angle eighty port, mean gyro angle about twenty-five left, torpedo depth set at six feet.

"Just before the first torpedo hit, the Japs must have sighted the wakes, for they could be seen running in all directions. Forty seconds after the first shot, the first torpedo was heard and observed to hit—directly beneath the large raked stack. Seven seconds later the second torpedo hit. The target was immediately enveloped in a cloud of heavy black smoke and flame, its bow dropped rapidly, and the ship took a list of about thirty degrees to port.

"Ordered full right rudder and full speed to get clear of the destroyer before its depth charges started going off. At range of about 400 yards, slowed to two-thirds speed and started taking pictures through the periscope.

"About two minutes after being struck, the destroyer's bow dropped under, the tail came out, with both propellers fanning the air, and about 200 Japs started clambering aft. No boats could have been launched. The tail now rose higher and higher, from thirty degrees to sixty, then finally, as the angle got steeper, they began dropping into the water like so many ants. All officers in the conning tower and half a dozen of the crew observed these last minutes of the enemy ship."[2]

When Sam was confident the area was clear of enemy airplanes and ships, he ordered surface conditions. In anticipation of finding many Jap survivors floating around—and as a precaution if some had guns, he ordered the men to break out the carbines and M-1s. But there wasn't a living soul in the water. The Japs had become victims of their own weapons—the tremendous concussion of forty or fifty depth charges going off like a string of Chinese firecrackers. We found nothing but mangled dead bodies and chunks of bodies floating in the water. We slowly cruised right through the midst of the macabre scene.

Sam's victory was more than one man's personal triumph; now the Navy brass would surely revamp its strategy for submarine warfare. The Japs were short of destroyers, and Sam figured that subs should concentrate on sinking what few were left, then the rest of the Jap Navy and merchant fleet would be at our mercy. And he was right.

Admiral Lockwood commented in his book: "Statistical reports showed that, up to this time, some sixty-four enemy DDs had been sunk. This left hardly enough to screen the Jap Fleet's heavy ships. Further reductions would leave them none for convoy escort duty. Admiral Nimitz, Commander-in-Chief, U.S. Fleets, figured that now was the time to concentrate on sinking destroyers and thus make enemy merchant ships—and major fleet units, as well—easier to attack."[3]

# 17

# Davy Jones Beckons

April 16 started with the dull prospect of another hot day patrolling the shores around the same old sun-drenched, jungle-covered island of *Woleai!* The name left a bad taste in everyone's mouth.

There wasn't much we could do to pass the time. To entertain ourselves we played cribbage, gin rummy, talked and drank coffee by the gallons. But on the morning of April 16, right after breakfast, the monotony was broken when the periscope watch officer made a sighting. Frank Lynch, the officer of the deck, passed down an urgent call for Sam to come to the conning tower.

Sam scurried up the ladder, and Carl pointed across the water's surface to a spot where, at a distance of about 6000 yards, a Jap medium cargo ship, estimated to weigh 3500 tons, was underway, just leaving the protection of Woleai's reefs.

Sam—as well as the rest of us—was ready for some action, after several days of impatient waiting. Lynch glanced through the periscope and discovered something new to sweeten the pot: Two *Fubuki* class destroyers were escorting the merchant ship, one to its port and the other to starboard.

He reported them to Sam, who chuckled and replied, "Really? Say, this is getting interesting. Those *Fubuki* destroyers are just our size. Maybe we can take another one."

"Yes, sir," answered Frank whose confidence was a bit shaken after another periscope peep. "But this time there's air cover, Captain. Moreover—moreover, whatever wind there was is dying down and the sea is getting glassy smooth."[1]

Frank was right; Sam agreed that the situation didn't look favorable for an attack. It was titillating, however, and Sam wasn't quite ready to back down from a fight, even if the odds were stacked against him. It was a matter he pondered carefully, as he reflected in his log entry:

"This picture stimulated the imagination. Here was a lightly loaded merchantman, heavily escorted by two large destroyers and provided with air coverage which was to remain until sunset! What made her valuable enough to justify such heavy protection? Were the Japs getting very, very short of cargo carriers? Or maybe they were being extra cautious since their proud new *Ikazuchi* destroyer didn't come back into port and was never heard from again! At any rate, our chances of getting another enemy combat ship looked good. Commenced trailing the targets at two-thirds speed and the chase was on!

"The convoy's first apparent base course was 270 (headed for Palau) and the AK was zigging radically, which gave her an advance of only six knots (she was making ten) along the base course. Our trailing speed of four knots enabled us to keep her in sight for a long time.

"1228—Smoke of the targets now just barely visible through the periscope, and Woleai atoll could no longer be seen astern. Surfaced with two engines on propulsion and one on a battery charge (our fourth engine was out of commission) and continued pursuit of the smoke."

Sam deliberately held back, waiting for nightfall and the aircraft that provided air cover for the convoy to return to their base. Three times he had to take the *Harder* under to avoid being spotted by the planes, but by nightfall the planes departed and the sub moved in closer to the convoy so as not to lose it.

"2300—Targets were now abeam to starboard at range of 15,000 yards. No evidence of enemy radar and nothing to indicate that they suspected our presence."[2]

During this time I circulated between the control room and the officers' wardroom, bugging everybody with a thousand questions. "What's going on?" "What's going to happen?" "How do we know where the tincans are going to be at 0330?" The answers gave me little comfort, we were going after the destroyers and merchantman, and Sam could only speculate about where they were heading.

Sam finally ordered the attack team to bed for some rest before the coming attack, and the watch and pursuit team relieved them. But Sam stayed on duty the entire time. Somehow I finally drifted off to sleep.

While the attack team slept, the second group kept abeam of the merchant ship and her two destroyer escorts. The three ships were continually changing positions in random, which kept Levin, Brock and Finney on their toes. The destroyers were not always registering pings on the sonar, which complicated matters. First one, then the other, would slow down its engines while the merchant ship passed it by. It was a tactic by which the slower-moving destroyer listened for the slow beat of submarine propellers, diving planes and pumps. The Japs were not dummies, and their constantly changing positions made it much more difficult to keep track of them.

Sam brought the *Harder* into position for an attack from the port side, which would keep the targets in the reflection of the moonlight on the water. But low clouds and intermittent rail squalls developed, killing any chance of seeing the targets silhouetted against the moon. Sam meticulously recorded in the *Harder's* log the details of trailing the convoy:

"2020—Merchantman contacted by radar at range of 29,000 yards. The night was not dark enough to attempt a surface approach, particularly with the thought in mind that the destroyers probably were equipped with radar; and there was insufficient visibility for a periscope attack before moonrise. Moonrise was scheduled for 0230; so decided to make a wide run around the enemy's port flank, track from ahead while figuring out his zigzag plan, and attack from his port bow at periscope depth with the targets sihouetted against the rising moon.

"2100—Settled down to a long night of it. Stationed tracking crew."[3]

By 0321 the overcast lifted to give Sam a clear shot from 3000 yards at the cargo ship. General Quarters was sounded and I jumped into action along with the rest of the crew. It was a busy time, with a myriad of orders going out all over the boat.

Sam wanted to take the cargo ship right then, but knew it might mean losing the two destroyers. He waited for a better shot, but the destroyer on the merchantman's port moved into a rain squall and was hidden from sight. Meanwhile, the other destroyer had disappeared. Sam decided to go after the merchantman, which by then was an easy shot at 1800 yards.

At 0335, Sam fired four bow torpedoes toward the ship. Here, from the *Harder's* log, is what happened next:

"About one minute after firing, I heard and saw one torpedo strike the cargo vessel just under its bridge. Flames and heavy black smoke shot up, covering the entire forward part of the ship. I shifted search then to the port quarter of the AK, hoping to find the destroyer. I didn't find it until one of the torpedoes did! A second explosion (nine seconds after the first) was seen and heard striking the destroyer.

"A large sheet of flame, similar to that made by the first torpedo, momentarily covered the destroyer, but the target was still in the rain squall and I could not tell where it was hit. "Timers" in the conning tower and both torpedo rooms now clocked both of the other torpedoes exploding at the end of their runs. The periscope was now swung back to the cargo ship which was furiously ablaze. Looked around for the other destoyer but it could not be seen. Ordered full right rudder to clear the torpedo tracks and went to deep submergence.

"Reached 300 feet before the depth-charging started. Received eight depth charges over a period of the next two hours. The propellers of the destroyer were heard to pass directly overhead three separate times, but its depth charges were released on only one of these occassions. None was too close and no damage was sustained."[4]

The next morning, Sam cautiously brought the *Harder* up to periscope depth. In the early dawn's light he peered through the periscope and saw the results of the night's attack. The sinking merchantman was sending up towers of brilliant white and almost smokeless flames. No survivors were seen. Sam continued to search, but was unable to spot either the stricken destroyer or the one which depth-charged the *Harder* during the night, so he claimed sinking only the merchantman and damaging one destroyer.

Throughout the depth-charging, the officers and men showed a coolness and courage I never dreamed possible. Sam never left the controls the entire time. Because we were running silently, the air grew hot and humid and Sam stripped down to his shorts and threw a towel around his neck to keep it handy for wiping perspiration from his face. Calmly and quietly he gave orders and directions for the continuous period of depth-charging. Later on, some of the men admitted to me that some explosions were very close.

When we finally surfaced after weathering this attack, Sam had the nerve to turn to me and ask: "Wouldn't you rather do that than dive in a plane through ack-ack fire?"

"No!" was my immediate and emphatic answer.

After leaving our calling card at Woleai, we deadheaded for Australia. The long, dull patrol was finally accomplished. Libertytown, here we come!

But 3300 miles is a long haul on a tiny submarine that at best will do only twenty-one knots. The days began to string out in monotonous repetition, each one as hot and empty as the one before it. Boredom came back to haunt us like an unwelcome ghost. What we needed was something different— anything to help beat the doldrums.

Diversion came each day during chow, while the third-string relief team was on a submerged training watch at the periscope and diving stations. On this occasion, Sam and I joined several other off-duty officers for lunch in the officers' wardroom.

The duties of the men on watch were standard. Every fifteen minutes they were to plane—or steer—the sub up to periscope depth, which was about fifty-five feet beneath the surface, and scan the horizon in all directions. If nothing alarming was sighted, the sub would be taken down again to 150 feet. It was very much a routine procedure.

But on this day, it would not be routine. No one was aware that we were silently inching closer and closer to death. Instead, some men were lounging around, others were at their duty stations, and still others, like Sam and myself, were enjoying that welcome diversion I mentioned earlier.

We had two cooks on board. J.W. Thomason, one of my rescuers, was the cook for the enlisted men, and Robert Moore was the cook for the officers. Robert, a robust black who stood six-foot three and weighed 205, had large white teeth and a wide, winning smile. I understood that he was a lay preacher in civilian life and I believed it too, because he brought his religion along into the Navy. When you engaged him in conversation back in the galley he was sure to salt his comments with insights on "my Jesus." It always fascinated me that

## Salvation for a Doomed Zoomie

Robert talked about Jesus Christ as if he knew Him intimately—like they were personal friends or something.

Robert had a keen sense of humor too. Every day he asked me what I wanted for dessert. No matter what I requested, I always got whatever he had prepared for that day—and it was usually canned fruit! It became a standing joke at chowtime.

Well, on this particular day, we were crammed tightly into the dinnette in the wardroom, finishing chow and talking about the usual things—the Japs, winning the war, girls, families and football.

Robert stuck his head in and asked in his melodic, southern drawl: "Mistah Galvin, what y'all want fo' dessert t'day?"

"Strawberry shortcake!—with lots of whipped cream."

My request brought the usual laughs from the other officers.

Robert just smiled with that big, toothy grin of his and responded: "Comin' right up, Mistah Galvin!" And with that, he turned and headed back toward the galley.

A few minutes later, he returned and presented me—and all the officers in the wardroom—with a dish of the usual canned peaches.

Moments later our minds were totally occupied with stowing away big helpings of dessert, for none of us had any inkling of the danger that was upon us.

For some unknown reason the incident was never recorded in the *Harder's* log. But years later Admiral Lockwood interviewed several crew members to piece together the dramatic events which took place, unknown to those of us in the wardroom. Even today, as I read his account of the peril, I shudder at how close we all came to death. Here, for you to read, is Admiral Lockwood's suspenseful version of the hair-raising, near tragic experience:

"As they neared the end of noonday chow, the *Harder*—unknown to all—was nosing deeper and deeper into depths where the pressures of the sea are too enormous for all but a few denizens of the deep.

"Second by potent second, the sub noséd downward from a periscope look. She was already far below the limits of her test depth—at a level so perilous that at any moment the terrific pressures of the mighty deep would close like jaws of steel and crush the *Harder* and all on board into pulp.

"But no one—not a living soul—aboard the *Harder* was aware of the terrible jeopardy in which they stood.

"Throughout the ship, men were eating or loafing or at their stations. In the control room, the still-inexperienced relief diving officer fought vigorously to force the ship down through what he thought was a layer of cold water—a dense, ping-proof stratum of low-temperature water beneath which subs like to seek sanctuary against pursuing destroyers.

"The diving officer was annoyed and puzzled. The needle on the diving dial stood firm at 120 feet despite his every effort. He had already flooded additional ballast water in the forward trim tank to give her more down angle. She took the angle all right, but the needle still hung at 120.

"'Flood auxiliary,' he ordered, with more than a touch of asperity, 'Damn her cranky soul, anyhow!'

"Every pound of water that entered might well have been a clod dropped on the lid of the *Harder's* coffin. Deeper she went. Moment by moment the almost unendurable pressures on the sub increased. The breaking point was creeping close.

"But no one aboard the *Harder* knew it. Back in the maneuvering room, Electrician's Mate, Second Class, Robert G. McNamara of Colorado Springs, one of the *Harder's* many plank owners, stood duty at main motor controls. Above his head was a depth gauge. The needle on the gauge was *not* at 120 feet. It had swung far over to the right—to the deep, deep depths that are out of bounds for mortal men and their puny creations.

"McNamara normally paid only casual attention to his depth gauge. The depth at which the submarine was running was no concern of his. That was handled in the control room.

Salvation for a Doomed Zoomie

His primary task was to be alert to increase or decrease speed on signal from the Diving Officer.

"McNamara was mildly wondering what took the *Harder* so long to level off when he happened to look up at the depth gauge. His thick crop of hair almost stood on end and deadly cold chilled his bare and sweat-shining back.

"'Holy mackerel,' he gasped, sudden fear almost choking him as he seized the intercom and shouted: 'Hey, control room, control room—what's up? My depth gauge is way over in the red—the needle is almost up against the stop!'

"In the control room—in torpedo rooms—in the wardroom—all over the ship—the warning cry was heard with heart-stopping effects. In the wardroom, Dealey and Lynch were on their feet and headed for the nearby control room before most of the shocked hearers realized what had been said. Sam took a running squint at the depth gauge in his cabin. What he saw almost made his blood congeal! Big and heavy as he was, Frank had a running start on his skipper. He reached his long-familiar diving station a moment ahead of Sam and took over.

"To bring the *Harder* back to a safe level from a depth so low that it cannot even be divulged for reasons of security was a tricky job that demanded skill, coolness, and above all, speed of decision.

"'All back, emergency!' was the order McNamara received in the maneuvering room. 'Blow bow buoyancy....pump auxiliary to sea' were the orders given in the control room while all hands held their breath and watched the main ballast pressure gauges—the only depth-indicating gauges which appeared to be working. The hiss of high-pressure air, the chatter of the trim pump, and the thrumming of the propellers trying desperately to pull the ship back from oblivion were the only sounds in the compartment.

"None dared to speak. Everyone was listening for the first terrifying crack of steel plating which would spell their doom.

206

Gradually the forward motion of the ship was reversed; slowly the bow came up; and with agonizing hesitancy the pressure in the ballast tanks lessened.

"'Thank God!' was the audible murmur throughout the length of the ship.

"'What caused the near disaster? Who knows—a barnacle, a leak, a hostile gremlin—any one of them could have caused the depth gauges to stick. Now, no one remembers the causality to the gauges, but one thing they will always remember is the name of a man—Robert G. McNamara—who, that day, saved his ship and his shipmates.'"⁵

Wouldn't you think that close call would bring old John Remarkable down to his knees for a word of prayerful thanks? Nope, not yet. Makes you wonder sometimes why the Lord just doesn't give up in disgust!

# 18

# Voyage Down Under

**B**y now I was standing watch at night up on the deck as the after deck watch officer. I'd put in my four hours there, then go down to the radio shack for another four to six hours of duty, coding and decoding radio messages. Everything had become routine. I was beginning to feel imprisoned in the sub, and that I was a slave to schedules: four hours topside, another stint in the radio shack, then eat, sleep, maybe play cribbage or gin rummy, or just talk—whatever I could discover to escape boredom.

The first happy promise of reprieve came on April 20. Frank Lynch informed the Skipper that the *Harder* had just enough fuel remaining in her tanks to make the 3300-mile trip to the nearest gas station—the American submarine base at Freemantle, Australia. There wasn't much choice: Sam would have to end the patrol the next day and head back. But before he did, he wanted to leave the Japs on the island something to remember him by. All of us wanted to get out of there in the worst way, but, like the skipper, we also thought it would be fun to leave a lasting impression on the Japs on Woleai.

The next day the *Harder* surfaced about 2000 yards off the beach. Ammunition was brought up on deck for the four-inch gun as well as the smaller 20-mm guns. Everybody was smiling in anticipation of giving those Nips a parting shot!

Most of the boat's action took place in the control room, and it was fascinating to watch all that went on. But the cramped quarters were no place for a sightseer, and I'm afraid I mostly just got in everyone's way.

It was a peaceful morning and the surface of the water was calm. The island was silhouetted in the early light of pre-dawn. The sun started to rise and Sam pointed the *Harder's* nose northwest, directly toward the island.

At 0627, Sam gave the command: "Commence firing!"

He didn't have to tell us twice. The peaceful tropical morning was shattered by the booming thunder of the four-incher and the chatter of the 20-mm guns. White smoke from the guns left an acrid smell that filled the air. Brass shell casings clattered across the deck, most of them dribbling over the side and splashing into the sea.

The assault really boosted our morales—especially the gunners. I don't know how much damage we inflicted on the Jap installations, but it sure started their day with a headache!

In less than two minutes from the time we opened fire, Tom Buckner's shrill whistle blew for cease fire. The diving klaxon squawked its warning as the gunners and ammo handlers hurriedly secured the guns and dived for the hatches. The *Harder's* nose slipped beneath the surface, and we were out of sight before the Japs even knew what hit them!

We thought it would be smooth sailing on to Australia after that. But not yet!

It happened during the midnight watch, just as we were passing through the Straits of Mulucca, enroute to Freemantle. Six of us were up on the bridge. It was a peaceful, calm night, and since we were so close to Australia, we felt confident that the Japs were far, far away. So to us, it was just another routine watch. We felt comfortable and relaxed—*too* comfortable and relaxed!

Then it happened. We heard a high-pitched, screaming whine that sent a chill up my spine. Then it disappeared. Every eye scanned the horizon for the source of the ominous sounds. We looked and looked, and then..."Torpedo!" yelled one of the lookouts, shattering the tranquil mood of the night.

My blood froze! And my eyes must have been as big as silver dollars, because there, charging straight for the *Harder's* midsection, was the telltale streak of white bubbles. Some torpedoes run true and level and others are erratic. This one was porpoising—rising to the surface, then diving deep, then coming back to the surface again.

There wasn't time to sound an alarm. I just sucked in my breath and grabbed hold of the rail to brace myself for the explosion.

"Here it comes!" I yelled, my knuckles turning white from gripping the rail so tightly. And the torpedo continued porpoising directly toward us at 40 knots.

A heart-beat.

Then a couple seconds.

Then...then....

Nothing happened!

"There it is!" yelled one of the men, and the rest of us did a one-eighty and saw the torpedo on the opposite side of the sub, heading away from us! By some incredible quirk of fate, that torpedo dove right underneath the *Harder's* keel, missed the sub entirely and kept on going!

After that, we searched and searched, but were unable to spot a Jap sub or ship or torpedo bomber. Where did the torpedo come from? No one knows.

Wow! What an incredible adventure for a cocky young Ensign named Galvin to have in only a few days! Shot down over the Pacific...bailed out at 350 feet...parachute torn open...swam five miles with no flotation gear...tangled with sharks...washed ashore on an enemy-held atoll...rescued by a maverick sub skipper at the risk of his boat and crew...escaped being hit by Jap snipers...the Fifth Fleet prolonging its offensive until I'm rescued...the sub I'm on is part of the bait for a Jap destroyer...the sub incredibly becomes the hunter instead of the hunted...the sub narrowly escapes being crushed at depths where no sub has ever before ventured...and we escape a run-away torpedo that comes out of nowhere and just happens to dive underneath us!

You would almost think there was some logic behind it all. More than once over the years that followed, I've been told: "Galvin, I think someone up there is looking out for you!" But I brushed off these kinds of remarks. Why would God single out *me*? Though I had to admit that to escape so many close calls with death seemed more than coincidental, I was reticent to attribute my mortal salvation to a God who was reaching out His helping hand. No, I reasoned, there had to be another explanation, a more rational one. So I kept on wondering, *why me*?

# 19

# Farewell at Freemantle

On May 3, 1944, thirty-three days after my rescue, the *Harder* reached Australia. We steamed up the Freemantle River to the American Sub Base at Perth, passing a myriad of factories, canneries, ship repair yards and docks crowded with throngs of cheering Aussies. Factory whistles were blowing and scores of fishing boats and other small craft escorted us in a grand procession up the river, tooting their horns and giving us a royal welcome! Even the seagulls that circled overhead seemed to be greeting us. It was *some* deal.

The *Harder* was auspiciously decked out for its arrival, proudly flying every flag that we could hoist. One small Jap flag was flown for every merchantman sunk, and there was a Jap pennant for each man of war. But the real eye-catcher was a "Zoomie Flag"—a crazy thing made by Tom Buckner and Phil Sampson that depicted some character in a life raft!

The *Harder's* gallant officers and enlisted men, wearing crisp khaki uniforms, lined the deck in precise military formation.

We passed in review near the docks of the sub base, then made a U-turn in the river and came back and maneuvered into the vacant dock that had been reserved for us.

There were three other subs at dock, and their sharp looking crews stood at attention in straight rows on the boats' decks.

Our boatswains threw hawsers to sailors on the dock, who quickly and skillfully moored us. The gangplank was lowered, and the inspection party walked up. They paused and turned aft before stepping aboard to present smart salutes to the American flag that was fluttering in the breeze. Then they saluted the officer of the deck and formally requested permission to come aboard, which, of course, was granted.

As the *Harder's* captain, Sam Dealey welcomed the party aboard, then turned sharply to lead them on the inspection rounds.

Rear Admiral Ralph Christie, Commander Submarines South West Pacific, was in the lead. A short, stocky man, he was followed by three other officers. I later learned they were sub skippers who were in Freemantle with their boats for reload of torpedoes, diesel, food and other supplies.

We were all lined up on deck for inspection, the enlisted men in two rows, facing each other, and aft, in a single row, the nine sub officers and myself. Admiral Christie was stern-faced as he slowly walked down the line of enlisted men, giving them a good looking over. Then he came over to us officers and began inspection at the opposite end of the line. Each officer's uniform was freshly pressed, without a wrinkle or speck of lint, and their shoes were spit-polished to a glossy sheen. Admiral Christie passed before the other ten officers without finding the smallest uniform infraction. Then he came to me.

I was a sight to behold, standing there in my khaki shirt, with no blouse, no tie, no insignia, no cap, no socks and pants that were too short.

215

"Well," he said, loud enough for everyone to hear and causing me to cringe, "My goodness sakes, what have we here?"

Through a deep blush I managed an embarrassed and apologetic smile—more of a nervous twitch of the corners of my mouth, really.

The rotund little admiral ambled right up to me, until we were standing there almost belly-to-belly. He looked me straight in the eye and said, "Don't you know that you're out of uniform? Don't you know that officers are supposed to wear ties at dress parade and otherwise be properly attired?"

"Yessir!" I blushed a deeper red.

The admiral turned to Sam and said, "Captain, what manner of flotsam and jetsam is this?"

"He's the zoomie, sir." And, Sam, sensing my discomfort, could hardly keep from bursting out laughing.

Well, right then, I sized up the situation and realized that the admiral knew about me all along. I sighed with relief.

The admiral chuckled and extended his hand. "Welcome aboard, Zoomie. I don't know who you are, or what it's all about, but you must be awfully important back on the *Bunker Hill*, because they've been sending wires about every three days, wanting to know where you are and when you're going to be sent back. But I'll tell you, Zoomie, I think you've earned a rest just as well as the rest of these submariners, so you go on up to the rest camp and I won't even report the sub in for a week. And then at the end of that week, I'll have to send you on. I'll cut coded orders for you, because you absolutely can't tell how or when you got here."

Following the inspection, the three sub skippers who were with Admiral Christie came up to me and said they hoped I would remember all my life what Sam Dealey had done for me—because if they had been in charge, I would have been left for saki stew meat! Then they gathered around Sam, anxious to learn more about his destroyer-sinking experience and tactics.

The rest camp was a small resort hotel which could accomodate maybe thirty people. All the officers except Dealey were there; he stayed in a separate little cottage—a special courtesy since he was a commanding officer, so we didn't see much of him.

The woman manager of the hotel said the place was ours: "Just make yourselves at home, boys, I've been instructed to give you whatever you want to eat and drink." That was good news to us!

We were usually up at nine or ten, had a big breakfast, lunched from one till two, then had dinner at eight. We literally lolled around and partied that whole time.

Our days were spent sun bathing, resting and sightseeing in Perth. It was fantastic! We were given all the drinks anyone could want (and sometimes more), and the food was terrific. At night we played cards, sang songs, drank lots of ale, told tall tales and talked about girls. The whole purpose of the stay was rest and relaxation—and *that* we did plenty of!

During that time, two notable things happened. On the second day someone came into my room and said, "Hey, Galvin, you're wanted on the phone."

I headed for the phone, wondering, *Why would anyone want me on the phone? No one in Perth knows me, and no one anywhere else even knows that I'm here!*

The man calling me identified himself as a captain, but I've long forgotten his name.

"Admiral Christie requests the presence of your company for lunch at his home on Thursday," he said, matter of factly. "Would you please attend?"

I didn't know what to say, so I put my hand over the phone's mouthpiece and yelled over to Frank Lynch: "Hey, Lynch, this is some captain on the phone, and he's inviting me to lunch at Admiral Christie's house. What should I tell him?"

"What do you ask me for? When an admiral requests something, it's an order! Tell him you'll be there!"

I did, and the captain said they'd send a car to pick me up.

When I got off the phone, Lynch told me that he and Sam Dealey would probably be invited too. "Relax, Galvin, and we'll all go over together."

But what would I wear? I still didn't have a regular uniform. I couldn't get any money in Australia to buy clothes, and since Perth was a surface navy town, no one had an aviator's uniform anyway. I thought about buying some civilian clothes, but the submarine supply officer said he couldn't give me any money because I didn't have my pay number.

As a last resort I went into town to the Australian Salvation Army. I must have told them a convincing sob story because they loaned me a hundred pounds on my promise to repay it. Since there were no naval aviator uniforms to be found in the city, I bought a pair of plain khaki trousers—that fit! At least I would look halfway presentable when I had lunch with the admiral.

I think it was Thursday, May 6, that the luncheon took place. The Navy car pulled up in front of the hotel right on time, and sure enough, Sam was in it. Lynch and I hopped in and the driver headed out to Admiral Christie's.

As we drove along, Sam said, "Now, Zoomie, don't be surprised at whatever goes on. This admiral's a real character, and you'll probably have a lovely lunch. Now this is important: If the admiral suggests that we shoot craps, you'd better volunteer!"

It all sounded a little irregular, but thanks to Sam's tip-off, I was ready for anything.

When we arrived, we were offered Tasmanian ale and then mingled with the rest of the luncheon guests (all high-ranking naval officers). After a while the admiral came down, and, to my surprise came directly over to where I was standing and chatted with me for a few moments. A steward announced that lunch was ready, and the admiral escorted me into the dining room. What followed was a fabulous seven-course feast!

218

After lunch, the admiral said, "Well, boys, this is all very nice. What do you say we roll back the carpet and I'll give you a chance to pay for your meal?"

Sam winked at me.

"By the way," Admiral Christie added, "before we get started at shooting craps, we have a little business to attend to, so if you'll all assemble out on the lanai."

We all went out and the admiral said, "We have a couple of citations to award." He started off with a citation for one of the other sub skippers. Then he told the story of my rescue to the gathering, making me out to be some sort of hero, which of course I wasn't.

The admiral turned to me and said, "Zoomie Galvin! Two steps forward, front and center."

I marched right up directly in front of him, self-conscious about all that gold braid surrounding me. And who wouldn't have been?—wearing what I had on! There I stood in my plain khakis, with no insignia, no nothing! I really felt out of place.

"We have a citation to read," the admiral announced. Then he pulled out a little card, and started to read: "Citation reads as follows: 'Presented to a gallant young aviator who went AWOL to join the submarines, then qualified in one patrol.'" Then he pinned the submarine combat award on me and gave me the card.

"Now, Zoomie," he said, "be sure and carry this card with you at all times, because you're going to get challenged by every submariner you meet when they see an aviator walking down the street with a submarine combat pin. Actually, there's no medal I'd rather own than that one myself. But now, of course, the Pentagon won't let me go on a sub into combat. So, I hope you'll wear that with pride, as long as you're in the naval service."

I assured him that I would, thinking how ridiculous to receive an award when I had gotten myself shot down and was little more than a hitch-hiker on board the *Harder*.

Then we went back inside the admiral's house. All of us got down on our knees on the floor, and I participated in my first and only game of craps!

The *Harder's* officers and I spent the rest of the week having pre-parties that were building up to the big farewell party they threw for me on my last night in Perth, which was May 9.

The farewell party could have gone on and on, but I had to leave. At five that morning, having had too little sleep and too much party, I boarded Australian airlines plane. I remember very little except that the *Harder's* officers poured me on the plane while we all sang boisterous songs.

My flight took me across Australia to Melbourne, Sidney and, finally, the army base at Brisbane.

I walked up to the flight operations desk, and the sergeant on duty, eyeing my strange uniform, asked, "Who are you?"

"John Galvin."

"Where are you going?"

"I don't know, but here are my orders."

Now this sergeant, who was kind of a loud-mouth, asked, "What do you mean you don't know where you're going?"

"I suggest you read my orders, sergeant."

He reddened up, then took my orders to the back room. A few minutes later an officer came out with my orders in hand and said, "We don't understand: What are you? Who are you supposed to represent?"

"Sir, I can't tell you; obviously my orders are coded. You're supposed to give me the earliest, highest priority out of here."

"Well, your orders certainly say that. You've got the highest priority, and we don't understand that. You're not even in uniform."

"Well, don't worry about that, just send me on."

The letter was convincing. Early the next morning, I reported back to board a converted Army B-24 to Pearl Harbor, arriving at the operations office without a single piece of luggage.

"The colonel's not gonna like this," shrugged the operations officer.

I didn't know what he meant until we went out to the plane and encountered the colonel. It turned out that I was bumping him. He had been in Australia for a couple of years and had not seen any combat duty. He had lived a soft life there and had grown pompous. I imagined what he would be like when he got back to the States—big hero comes home, no doubt!

But my priority was higher than his. At first he refused to give up his seat, demanding to know who I was that I could be bumping him. He swore at me, reminding me that he was a full colonel in the United States Army and all that sort of thing. He was upset and obnoxious.

The operations officer told him, "Nevertheless, colonel, this guy's got higher priority, and he's bumping you."

When I got into Pearl, it was the same treatment. Everybody wanted to know *who* I was and *what* I was. I couldn't tell them a thing, but I got immediate service. I was told to stay in a Quonset hut that night, not to leave, and that my meals would be brought into me.

The next morning I boarded another plane, this one to Kwajalein. From there I was flown back to the *Bunker Hill*.

During the thirty-eight-hour trip back to the *Bunker Hill*, I had ample time to think about all that had happened since I had flown off the carrier's deck that morning of April 1. It was nothing short of a miracle that I was alive and returning to my squadron.

The most vivid memory was my last conversation with Sam Dealey, the night of the farewell party. I still get goose-bumps when I recall his words: "Zoomie, I want you to remember all the rest of your life about the wind and the tide and the current—that they carried you ashore. Never in my entire naval career have I ever seen anything like it. You had a lot of help going for you that day. So don't you forget it."

*Salvation for a Doomed Zoomie*

It was then Sam related that he had asked Admiral Raymond Spruance to continue providing air cover while he and the *Harder's* crew rescued me. I was dumbstruck as Sam continued: In order to comply with his request, Admiral Spruance prolonged for two and a half hours the attack by the entire fleet of 110 warships, including sixteen carriers!

It was crazy! Think of the potential *loss of life* and *planes* and equipment! Approximately 150,000 to 200,000 men were involved, just to save one single life! Think of the cost—bombs, ammunition, aviation gas, diesel fuel. Absolutely preposterous! Admiral Spruance could have been court-martialled or at least relieved of command for making such a decision.

Sam Dealey was no less foolhardy. He risked his thirty million dollar sub and eighty-four mens' lives when he put that sub up on the reef to rescue me.

I know today that all the circumstances surrounding my rescue were not mere coincidences. Hitting the tail of the plane at better than 250 m.p.h., the chute opening without any help from myself, the wind, the tide, the current, Sam Dealey and the *Harder*, Admiral Spruance's order to hold up the fleet—hardly coincidences! There was a plan behind it all—a divine plan, orchestrated by God Himself, who wanted me to be rescued. Why? Why me? Others died! And therein lies the real reason why I never told this story—why me? It's a question that I have asked myself for many years. And only recently has the answer begun to unfold.

# 20

# Reunion at Sea

My return to the *Bunker Hill* sparked a great reunion with all the guys in the squadron. I felt a little sheepish at first because of my blunder in getting shot down, but none of the guys ribbed me about it. That's not to say there wasn't some joking around, though— mostly to cover-up any sentimental feelings, I'm sure. Like Peedy Boyles: He said he was sorry to see me back because he would have to move back to the upper bunk.

The warmest welcome came from Gus, T.I. and Chris. The four of us were such a close-knit team that we felt almost as if we were kin. They greeted me as if I were the prodigal son.

My most anxious moment was when Commander Collins came up to the ready room and welcomed me back. But to my surprise (and relief), he didn't have a single word of reprimand.

Even the Catholic chaplain was there. He came up to me with tears in his eyes and asked if I could ever forgive him.

"For what?" I asked. Then he recalled that when it was announced I had been shot down, he prayed for God to forgive him. He feared that his remark about the Navy serving steak and eggs and my not eating again that day before a perilous mission had somehow condemned me and he worried that I would never forgive him. I'd forgotten all about it, but I forgave him anyway, and this seemed to take a heavy load off his conscience.

Things had changed in the time I had been gone from the *Bunker Hill*—not with the others so much as with me. It was my attitude. Prior to getting shot out of the sky, my ego was so great I thought no one could touch God's gift to the war effort. But my experience had been humbling and sobering. I'd been shot down once, and it could happen again. But maybe next time I wouldn't come back.

After returning, one of my first missions was a sortie over the island of Guam on June 14. Just before our pre-dawn take-off, in the routine intelligence briefing, we were told to expect stiff opposition from the Japs, who were concentrated on Orote Penninsula. Intelligence had no idea how many rifles or machine guns would be shooting at us, but they did give us estimates on the types and numbers of enemy planes. They also said we would encounter more than 500 anti-aircraft guns of three inch bores and greater. That is a dense concentration of guns, considering that Orote Penninsula is only two to three miles long and a half mile wide. Anticipating that much opposition was a little unsettling.

We flew in before sunrise from 25,000 feet, and just as we pushed over into our vertical dive, the ground lit up like a Christmas tree. *Look at the fools*, I thought, *They're turning on all the lights for us!* Then I realized that those weren't electric lights at all, but rather the open ends of gun barrels spitting death at us! And there I was, flying right through that shower of fire. We lost some good men there, and it's incredible that I got through it unscathed.

## Salvation for a Doomed Zoomie

A few months later, on September 21, 1944, our flight—Gus, T.I., Chris and I—was in the first group of fighters that were sent in on a major strike against Manila. No American planes had flown over Manila since MacArthur left in 1942. With sixteen carriers launching twelve to sixteen planes each—a total of over 200 planes, we were a relatively big wave of fighters—all converging on the primary target of Clark Field and Manila.

We arrived to discover that the Japs had barrage balloons up. To us, going after balloons was like shooting sitting ducks, and we gave them a good spraying with our machine guns. But just when we thought things were going to be easy that day, down came the Zeros to get us. How many there were, I don't know, but they easily had us outnumbered. They were the older-type "Oscars" of the Japanese Army—the Ki-43 built by Nakajima, but their vintage hardly affected the determination of the pilots: they came at us like a swarm of angry hornets, attacking from every direction. We quickly got on the offense and went after them. The dogfight was on, and the radio crackled with the shouts and warnings of pilots reporting the location of the Oscars to the others.

During the melee I got on the tail of an Oscar and stayed glued to him as he tried to out-run me in a steep dive. He couldn't shake me loose, though, and I got a lead on him and peppered him good. That's all it took.

Japanese planes had little armor plating and were not using self-sealing gas tanks as we did, so when you scored a good hit, you could generally count on setting the target on fire. The plane I hit was no exception: It burst into a flaming torch and arched toward the ground. It's crash created a huge mushrooming cloud of fire and smoke.

Seconds later I spotted another Oscar. It was flying down low, headed for a landing at Clark Field, which indicated it was probably damaged or low on gas. I swung down and got it in my sights, blasted away and splattered it as it flew only a few feet off the ground, along a hedge row. It bellied into the ground, sliding and digging a long furrow, then exploded.

I climbed back up to the clouds, looking around for more targets, but finding none. Then I spotted an F6F and joined up with it. We flew side-by-side back to the carrier. After landing I found out the pilot was George Kirk, from Moline, Illinois. I think he bagged three Japs that day.

There was great elation over shooting down Jap planes—like scoring a touchdown in football. We were trained to do this. Nothing personal—we never saw the pilots unless they bailed out. We were shooting at airplanes. We were taught that Japs were the enemy, and that we were to hate them and to shoot them down. Not once did I feel remorseful about killing; I don't recall any of our pilots expressing regret (though they might have had secret feelings).

On October 16, we catapulted off the *Bunker Hill* for an escort and bombing run over Formosa. I was in the first flight sweep of twenty-four fighters from several carriers, which probably included the *Lexington, Wasp, Hornet* and *Franklin*. Our primary mission was to blast in there and try to shoot down all the enemy planes so that the following waves of planes coming in could bomb the airfield and a large aircraft factory at Matsuyama Field.

As we dived down out of the overcast sky, we were immediately jumped by about eighty Jap Tojos, a new frontline fighter that was comparable to our F6F in firepower, armament and armor. The Tojos were *everywhere*, darting back and forth in pursuit, bent on bagging some Hellcats. But I eluded them like a slippery fish in wet grass, eventually finding sanctuary in a cloud.

Maybe a minute later I poked my nose out of the clouds, only to encounter more Jap planes—*only* Jap planes; not one of ours was in sight. Almost as a reflex I started shooting. The action was so harried and fast that most of what happened is a blur in my memory.

227

I spotted a Tojo and went full throttle after it, concentrating on getting it in my sights. When I had the plane locked in, I blasted away and zapped it. Then I looked for another one. They weren't hard to find, because they were looking for us, too!

I saw a distant plane coming head-on for me. I slouched down in my seat and peered through the gun sight. Just as I was about to squeeze the trigger, I heard Gus' voice over the radio:

"Dumbo, do you have a plane coming at you head-on?"

"I sure do!"

And at that split second, we both realized that we were headed at each other! A second later and we would have fired at each other, no doubt shooting each other out of the sky.

Boy! What a relief when Gus called! Both of us sort of thought the opposite plane was an F6F, but the new Tojos resembled the F6F when seen head-on. Good old Gus! What a welcome sight!

Before the dogfight was over I succeeded in knocking three Tojos out of the sky. This brought my total number of victories to five. Altogether that day, we came out of there alive with fifty-two claimed Jap planes shot down and no Americans lost!

On our next mission, Gus and I were on a 300-mile search for the Jap fleet. As we neared the area where we expected it to be located, I spotted the first enemy plane high above us, just below the cloud layer.

"Topsy! Twelve o'clock high!" I yelled excitedly over the radio to Gus. Topsy was the code name for an an old American-made DC-2 that we had sold to the Japs before the war. I had forgotten it carried no guns, and I could have closed in slowly for the kill. But I bore down on it, shooting away like crazy, and in my excitement to beat Gus there, pushed ahead full throttle and overran it. I looked back over my shoulder as I circled around, and saw that the plane was in flames. Seconds later, Gus closed in and finished the plane off. Chalk one up for good old Gus!

A few minutes later Gus ordered me to fly above the cloud layer, and he stayed below.

Moments later he called me over the radio: "Hey, Dumbo, make a diving left turn through the clouds and come in shootin'."

I did, and it was unbelieveable. It was just like a picture story book. There were three Nells flying in close V-formation. Nells were the old twin-tailed, eleven-passenger Jap high level bomber.

I came through the clouds and was right on top of them. I came in on a "beam" run—from the left side, but a little above them, and set my sights on the lead plane, really drilling it. In the early morning sun that poked through the clouds I saw the glitter of the plexiglass when it plopped out. The Nell lurched and started a nose dive, leaving a trail of black smoke, and I was sure I had gotten the pilot.

Then I switched targets to the nearer of the two remaining planes. I was hitting it good; the left prop stopped and then the right landing gear dropped down, and the Nell was on fire. Gus saw what was happening and came in behind me and finished off the Nell.

I turned my attention to the last of the three Nells. Its gunner was throwing everything he could at me as I bore down, peppering his plane with machine gun fire. I was coming in too fast, though, and overran the plane, pulling up at the last possible second, missing the twin tails by the skin of my teeth! Then the Nell started to turn away. I kept zigzagging back and forth to slow down so I could come back in for another shot. Meanwhile, Gus finished off Nell number two. I finally slowed down enough to move in on Nell number three. I got it in my sights and sprayed it good with my 50s. It exploded in a ball of flames, and plummetted downward.

After a raid, an F6F's wings are folded back to conserve deck space.

On October 18, I was flying an escort and bomb run over the island of Luzon when, far below, we spotted some small Jap ships. Gus and I peeled off and went down first, but missed. Then I went in on a shallow angle dive called a skip bombing run on a 6000 ton transport. I steadily fired six of my guns as I closed in, then, just before I had to pull up to keep from crashing into the ship, I dropped my bomb. Brown, who was following me, verified in his report after the mission that I had hit the transport, and that he had seen it settle, stern-first.

When I first arrived in the South Pacific, many new Navy procedures were being implemented because of the acceleration of the war effort. Of particular interest to me was the policy that a carrier based squadron would fly twenty-five missions or remain in the war zone for six months. After that

John Galvin

a pilot was relieved and sent back to the States to rest. There he would be assigned to a new squadron or given Stateside duty as an instructor.

I should point out that, while the Army and Marines counted every flight as a mission, the Navy only counted those flights as missions in which there was combat. That's why we had so many flights. During one period, the ship never dropped anchor for 138 days at sea. Get here, get there—we would go in and get one place and clobber it, then retire back 300-400 miles, or as much as 500-800 miles. Tankers, ammunition ships and supply ships would meet us. All these materials would be transferred by lines from supply ships to the carrier. We did this with aviation gasoline, bombs, food, mail—everything.

I had fifty-five days of combat flying, spread from March 10, 1944, when we boarded the *Bunker Hill*, until October 26, when we were detatched. During that time I flew ninty-six combat missions, but that was fewer than average because of the lengthy time I was grounded—more correctly submerged—aboard the *Harder*. (Lamoreaux, I think, was up to 120 or 125 missions!) Perhaps one reason why the stress of combat didn't affect me like it did some of the others was because I had flown fewer missions. And believe me, the stress was heavy.

By this stage of combat experience, all the heroics were out of our minds, and dreams of conquest, Medals of Honor and the big Hollywood vision were no more.

It seemed that everytime we attacked a target somebody would get shot down. Probability says that the more missions flown, the greater the odds of getting shot down. I purposefully never dwelled on this, because if I had, I would never have taken off from the deck of the carrier in the first place. Some of the guys let the thought of death really get to them, and it shattered their nerves—combat fatigue it was called, and to those of us who saw it first-hand, it was a very real psychological condition.

232

An increase in the accident rate began to take place during landings and take-offs. Some of the pilots got careless in the air, and they became dangerous to themselves and to others around them. The problem often showed up at take-off time. A pilot might imagine hearing strange sounds in his engine and thus abort his flight.

Finally the ship and air group flight surgeons exercised their authority by not permitting pilots with combat fatigue to fly anymore.

Why some men got combat fatigue and others didn't was a complicated matter. The causes usually involved personal problems—not uncommonly subconscious fears and stress, and most of us never knew each others' feelings.

While combat fatigue wasn't a problem for me, I could relate with those who were plagued by it. It was a little like when I bailed out at sea and was trying to swim to shore: a time came when I was ready to accept the thought of drowning. In the same way, pilots suffering from combat fatigue came to believe they were not going to return from the next mission.

Why some could handle stress well and others had difficulty was a mystery. Some of the admirals, generals and politicians discounted combat fatigue as cowardice, but I don't think "manliness" had anything to do with it. Some of the men had never faced any major trials. Some had such smooth family lives that they did not know how to accept adversity. Others had never seen death, and they became fearful of dying and what was beyond life.

As for me, I had come very close to death when I was down at sea, and maybe it was that experience that somehow fortified me against an abnormal fear of dying, and I was able to continue flying.

The military still is trying to discover what makes a man a fighter pilot—how he is influenced by his psychological make-up and family background.

Right after the Palau attacks, Admiral Spruance was ordered back to Pearl Harbor. He was replaced by Admiral "Bull" Halsey who said it was nonsense for pilots to be relieved after only twenty-five missions or six months of combat duty. By that time, he believed, pilots were just starting to earn their salt. To him, combat fatigue was a bunch of hooey.

To us pilots, combat fatigue was a very real psychological malady. We saw it emotionally cripple some of our best buddies—and, in some cases, kill them. As for the number of missions, most of us felt that we could handle more than twenty-five, but that six months of stepped-up activity was about long enough.

Late in my series of combat missions, I was coming in on a flat downhill dive at a Jap ship, strafing all the way in, until I was close enough to release a bomb. All six guns were belching out death to the ship, when suddenly, without warning, all six guns jammed! Now, having one gun jam isn't uncommon, but to have all six jam at the same time is incredibly rare. What happened next took place in the twinkling of an eye. Though I was tense and keyed-up over diving down at 300 m.p.h. into the shower of bullets the Japs were spraying at me, in a split second I instinctively stooped forward and down to the right to punch the gun charger buttons to clear the jam.

*Crack!* The inside of the cockpit exploded in a shower of splinters of glass, accompanied by the shrill whistle of rushing air.

*What the...?*

I jolted upright in my seat and looked straight ahead. My gun sight was *shattered*! And most of my windshield had been blasted away! I strained my head to look behind me. There was a bullet hole in my headrest. A Jap shell equivalent to our .50-caliber had entered the cockpit through the windshield and lodged in my head rest! Less than a second before the shell hit, my eye had been in front of that gun sight.

Later on the implication of what had happened dawned on me. I was 2000 to 2500 feet out from the ship since I had not released the bomb yet, and since the Jap bullet was probably traveling at the rate of approximately 1200 feet per second, *that shell had to have already been in the air and on its way toward me when my guns jammed.*

I was so shaken up that I don't remember whether I hit the pickle to drop my bomb. All I could think about was my close call. Once again, I had survived.

What had made all six guns jam at that exact moment? A coincidence? Or divine intervention?

# 21

# Fate of the *Harder*

The day finally arrived for Fighter Squadron Eight to be relieved. There was no question that the war had taken its toll on our squadron. We ended up with one-third of our men lost, one-third grounded and one-third still flying.

We all looked forward to returning home to the States. That was the Navy's *usual* procedure: Relieve a squadron, send it home for some rest, then reform the squadron and send it back into the war zone.

Back at Freemantle, Sam Dealey and I had been talking about how the time was approaching for my squadron to be relieved and sent home. He gave me the telephone number and address of his wife, Edwina, in Santa Monica, and asked that I call on her when I got back.

We didn't get back to the States quite as fast as expected. Instead of being sent home right away, our squadron left the *Bunker Hill* to take up residence on some stinking little island called Ponam, off New Guinea.

It was there that I was surprised to receive a letter from Sam's wife. We had never met, of course, and she knew me only through Sam's letters, so it struck me as rather odd that she would write. I felt uneasy as my nervous fingers opened the envelope. It was a short letter, and she simply said, in cryptic to get through censorship, that *Sam was overdue and presumed lost*! I couldn't believe what I was reading. Sam Dealey—*lost at sea*! Impossible! Not Sam; there wasn't a Jap ship ever built that could sink the *Harder*! Experience taught us, though, that when a sub is overdue, it is sunk.

But as I read on, I discovered that Mrs. Dealey had received reliable information—through the Navy wives' "intelligence service," an underground communications network that had a reputation for amazing accuracy.

"You'll soon be going through Pearl Harbor," her letter continued, "would you please go over to Sam's place and see what you can find out. I really would appreciate it."

I immediately wrote back to her and related all the details about my rescue and the friendship that had developed between Sam and me. And I promised that I would find out as much as I could about Sam and the *Harder*.

Just as her Navy wives' "intelligence service" had predicted, *in less than a week*, my squadron was in Pearl Harbor. I had a sinking feeling about Sam's fate—yet one of disbelief that the sub could be lost. I let my imagination roam, thinking what it might have been like for Sam and the others to get crushed from the concussion of depth charges and lie in a watery grave in the dark depths at the bottom of the Pacific Ocean. The thought of it was almost more than I could bear. But I had to know for sure; I had to get the official word from the Navy itself.

The direct approach was the only one I could think of, so I waltzed around from Ford Island over to the sub base. What I hadn't realized was that the sub base at Pearl Harbor was headquarters for the entire Pacific submarine fleet. The head honcho—Admiral Lockwood—was there with the war room and all the intelligence facilities and staff.

I walked over to the administration building and was confronted by a tough-looking Marine sergeant at the gate. I told him I wanted some information about a sub, and he directed me inside where a lieutenant commander was seated behind a reception desk.

I told the officer that I understood the *Harder* had been sunk, and, like a dumb cluck, said that Sam's wife had asked me to learn what I could about her husband's disappearance.

He looked at me with a squint of suspicion and said: "I don't know what you're talking about."

"Surely you've heard of Sam Dealey and the *Harder*, commander. I just want to know what happened."

"I don't know what in the heck you're talking about."

I showed him the letter from Sam's wife. He only glanced at it, then handed it back.

"Well, I don't know who Mrs. Dealey is, and I don't have the slightest idea what you're talking about."

I was starting to get a little hot under the collar, and even though he out-ranked me, I blurted out, "Now, look commander, I know what I'm talking about. You're being evasive, and I'm going to stay here until I find out what I want to know."

"Okay, okay," he said, apologetically, a little surprised by my outburst. "I'll see what I can find out. Meanwhile, stay right here and *don't leave*."

He turned and started walking up the steps of an impressively large marble staircase. At the top landing, he disappeared down a hallway.

I sat down and waited. More than a half hour went by, and I was getting antsy. I got out of the chair and started wandering around. I started for the door, thinking I'd go outside and get some fresh air. The Marine guard, rifle in hand and stern-faced, stepped in front of me, blocking the doorway, and said, "Sir, you are not leaving."

"What do mean I'm not leaving, *sergeant*?" I emphasized his rank to remind him he was talking to an officer.

"I have orders to keep you here...*sir*," he said with a tinge of defiance.

"What? Hey, what kind of a chicken outfit is this, anyway?"

"Go back and sit down, *sir*!" he said firmly.

So I went back and sat down.

After almost an hour, down the stairs walked the lieutenant commander. "John," he said—and I detected his whole attitude had changed, "there is only one man who can talk to you, and he'll see you right now."

I followed him back up the stairs, then down to the second deck—which was, judging by all the shingles hanging over all the doorways, offices of high-ranking naval officers.

"In there," he said, motioning toward an open door. Then he called in to a man inside, who I couldn't see: "Charles, this is Lt. John R. Galvin."

I started to say, "Hello, Charles," to the unseen man inside, but just then he came around the corner. I saw that the arm of his coat had gold braid almost up to his armpit! I gulped. "Charles" turned out to be Vice Admiral Charles A. Lockwood, Commander, Submarines, Pacific Fleet.

*Now, what have I gotten myself into?* I thought. Nervous as all get out, I started to walk into the office, but stumbled, dropped my hat, got all flustered and very awkwardly did the only thing I could think of doing: I saluted. And that only embarrassed me more, because then I remembered that a Navy officer only salutes when he has his hat *on*—not like an Army officer who always salutes, regardless of hat.

The admiral just grinned at me. "Zoomie," he said, "sit down and *relax*, will you?"

Then he started talking to me about Sam Dealey. He got a little choked up and tears welled up in his eyes. He told me that Sam was surely lost. As he talked it became clear that Sam had been his protege.

The admiral brought me up to date on the *Harder's* activities. Right after I had said farewell to Sam and the crew, the sub went out on another combat patrol, accomplishing some incredible victories. Five destroyers were sunk in only six days, and this, according to the admiral, earned the *Harder* a Presidential Citation and brought Sam even more acclaim as one of the U.S. Navy's greatest sub skippers of all time. His gallantry earned him the Medal of Honor; five Navy Crosses (the Navy's highest award for valor); and, the Army Distinguished Service Cross, awarded by General Douglas MacArthur.

It is military custom to pull officers so heavily decorated out of combat, the rationale being that they had done their parts. But Sam Dealey and the *Harder* would not rest on their laurels, and put out to sea again, on their sixth combat patrol. Like all their previous patrols, this one was also successful: They sank two or possibly three more Jap destroyers.

Admiral Lockwood told me what he could about the *Harder's* last patrol, that fateful incident that sent Sam Dealey and more than eighty crewmen and officers to the bottom of the ocean. Details were sketchy at that time, but several years later, in 1949, Lt. Cmdr. Edward Beach, U.S.N., exhaustively researched the incident and wrote this account in *Blue Book* magazine:

"On the morning of August 24, 1944, *Harder* dived off the west coast of Luzon, in company with U.S.S. *Hake*. Dealey, being the senior skipper, had decided to make a reconnaissance in this area....

"Shortly after daybreak on the fateful twenty-fourth of August, echo ranging was heard, and two escort type vessels were sighted, both fairly small, of about one thousand tons each. Both submarines immediately commenced approaching for an attack. However, the larger of the two ships suddenly zigged away and entered an indentation in the coast line known as Dasel Bay. The other stayed outside, and at this time *Hake* broke off the attack, feeling the remaining target was hardly worth the torpedoes it would take to sink him. *Harder*, however, held on, and *Hake* sighted her periscope crossing in front, passing between *Hake* and the enemy vessel.

"*Hake* by this time had commenced evasive maneuvers, for the Jap was echo ranging loudly and steadily in her direction. Exactly what was in Sam Dealey's mind is, of course, not known; his previous record indicated that he would have had no hesitancy in tangling with this chap, if he thought it worth while. Furthermore, he had more or less gotten *Hake* into this spot, and may have felt that he owed it to the other submarine to get her out again. But whatever his motives, it appears that he maneuvered *Harder* between the other two vessels, with the result that the Jap, naturally enough, took off after him instead of after *Hake*. According to the latter's report, the enemy vessel showed some confusion, probably due to there being two targets where he had no reason to suspect more than one.

"Sam Dealey was perfectly capable of an act of self-abnegation such as this maneuver of his appears to have been. However, it must be pointed out that the enemy vessel concerned was a small anti-submarine type, hardly more than a mine-sweeper, and that he had several times previously come off victorious in encounters with much more formidable ships than this. Of the two submarines, *Harder* was doubtless the better trained and equipped to come to grips with this particular enemy. It was simply the fortunes of war that, in this case, fate dealt out two pat hands—and Dealey's wasn't good enough.

"With *Hake* a fascinated spectator, the Jap made his run. Possibly *Harder* fired at him, though *Hake* heard no torpedo on her sound gear. At any rate, the mine-sweeper came on over Sam Dealey, and suddenly dropped fifteen rapid depth charges. *Harder's* periscope was never seen after that, nor were his screws heard again.

"According to the Japanese report of the incident, the periscope of a submarine was sighted at about two thousand yards, and a depth-charge attack was immediately delivered. After this single attack, a huge fountain of oil bubbled to the surface, and considerable quantities of bits of wood, cork, and other debris came up and floated in the slick.

"So perished a gallant ship, a gallant captain, and a gallant crew. All of Sam Dealey's skill and daring could avail him not one iota against the monstrous fact that the enemy's first depth-charge attack, by some unhappy stroke of fate, was a bull's-eye."[1]

Thus Sam Dealey, the man who was willing to lay down his life for another, passed not into oblivion, but into the hearts of all submariners everywhere, and his name will always be mentioned when submarine warfare is discussed. Even today, tears fill my eyes when I think of this soft spoken Bible-reader and father of three children, whose body, entombed with his crew within the mangled remains of the *Harder*, lies at the bottom of the South China Sea.

Well, back to the story of my visit with Admiral Lockwood. We talked for an hour and a half, until he finished by saying, "Zoomie, I know you are going back to the States. Would you do me a favor? I am going to have my aide go down and collect personal effects—pictures and such of Sam Dealey and the *Harder*. Would you go call on Mrs. Dealey in Santa Monica? Take these mementoes to her and express my sincere gratitude and sympathy."

He said he'd extend my leave to do this. I told him that wasn't necessary.

"By the way," he said, "you surely must want some mementoes, too." Then he told the lieutenant commander to take me down to the photo lab and let me have any pictures concerning Sam and the *Harder* that I wanted.

When I got back to the States I called on Mrs. Dealey, and presented her with the packet of mementoes. This lovely,

*Salvation for a Doomed Zoomie*

Cdr. Samuel David Dealey

244

gracious lady fought back tears as I related what Admiral Lockwood had told me.

After my thirty days leave, I went back to the reformed Fighting Squadron Eight at Watsonville Auxillary Naval Air Station, which was a satellite field of NAS Alameda. By then I had been promoted to Lieutenant, Senior Grade, as were Brown and several other pilots in the squadron. Many new junior officers checked into the squadron, and I was one of a handful of senior pilots.

We were sent back to Puunene, then on to Saipan, where we boarded the U.S.S. *Hornet*. We were part of a huge air, sea and ground force that was preparing for the final assault on Japan. The horror of this impending operation was staggering: We were told an estimated one- to two-million Japanese and allies would die! But before we resumed combat, the atom bomb was dropped on Hiroshima, August 6, 1945, and on Nagasaki two days later. An estimated 200,000 Japanese were killed by those two bombs—a fraction of the casualties that would have resulted had the conventional assault taken place. Moreover, the atom bomb brought an immediate and early end to the war. Millions of American servicemen and women got down on their knees and thanked God that the war was over.

I was eligible for immediate discharge and took a fifty-five day trip back home on a liberty ship from Saipan. We docked at Philadelphia Naval Base, then went on to NAS Great Lakes at Chicago to be discharged. Though the long war was finally over and I was going home, the loss of Sam Dealey and the crew of the *Harder* left me in no mood to celebrate our country's victory.

# 22

# After The War

To my surprise, I learned after the war that some of my friends from among the *Harder's* officers and crew had for various reasons missed the sub's fateful sixth patrol. Among those who fate passed over were Frank Lynch and two of the men who rescued me, J. W. Thomason and Francis X. Ryan.

On leaving the Navy, Frank went to work for the Electric Boat Company at New Haven, Connecticut, where he was in charge of new sub design. I had dinner at his home about ten years ago. He had lost an eye in a car accident, but otherwise had changed very little since the war. It was Frank who gave me copies of the *Harder's* log.

I have not seen Thomason in person since the war, but did see him on the Navy's "Silent Service" film for television that re-enacted my rescue.

I had a letter from Francis Ryan a few months ago; he is retired and living in Florida.

I've attended numerous reunions of Fighter Squadron Eight, and therefore kept in contact with some of my flying companions.

Commander Collins scored nine victories during the war. Afterwards he stayed in the Navy for a few years and attained the rank of captain. He later resigned his commission and went into business with a national hotel chain. The last time I saw him was at one of our squadron reunions. He passed away in the late-1970s.

Peedy, my soft-spoken bunkmate on the *Bunker Hill*, returned to civilian life in Karnes City, Texas. He started a supermarket business called "Speedy Peedy's." He is now retired and lives on a ranch in Texas.

Chris Allen lives in Rockport, Texas.

Whitey Feightner stayed in the Navy and went on to become an admiral. McCuskey ended the war with fourteen victories. Allen got one, Brown three, and Gus six.

Brown died a few years ago, and several others have since passed away. It would be great to make contact again with those who are still around, and perhaps this book will help reestablish that contact.

Sam Dealey's wife, Edwina, refused to go to Washington to receive Sam's Medal of Honor. She was bitter that Sam had been permitted to return to combat (though he had demanded to return, insisting he had earned the right to lead a wolf pack). Edwina Dealey never recovered from her grief. While still a young woman, she died of a broken heart. The Dealey children, at last report, now live in the Dallas, Texas area.

# 23

# Threatening Skies and Stormy Seas

At the war's end, I was ready to return to civilian life and live out my dream of starting a career and raising a family. Months earlier I had married Claire, the girl I dated during my college years at Northwestern. I remember how good it was to be home with my bride—and the rest of my family, Mom and Dad and my two sisters. With peace at hand and my loved ones comfortable and happy, the future looked promising and bright.

My younger sister Helen had married Bob Eisenhart before the war started, while he was still in college. Bob served in Marine aviation during the war. When the fighting stopped Helen and Bob moved around for a while, then settled down in Petersburg, Illinois, where Bob, a chemical engineer, worked with the environmental protection agency. They soon had two fine children.

My other sister, Mary, became a captain in the WACs during the war. When peace came she married Cliff Quakenbush, a Marine veteran who saw action at Guadalcanal. They continued to live in Burlington and were blessed with two lovely daughters.

I went into a sales training course at the Vulcanized Rubber & Plastics Co. in Morrisville, Pennsylvania, making about half what I had been paid in the military. In a short time I became sales manager, and was there for twelve years. After that I went with a small plastic outfit in New York City for a year and a half.

Then Wes Westgaard and I started a plastics moulding business in Vermont. Wes was technically oriented, and I had some strengths in sales and administration. Together we made a good team, and our hard work rewarded us with a successful company and better than average profits.

One the most gratifying things I saw develop during that time was the relationship between Mom and Dad: their marriage deepened with warmth, commitment and understanding. Maybe it was because Dad had been attending church with Mom. Sadly, death took Dad in June, 1958 and I missed him more than I thought I would. Mom missed him too, but she was not alone—not with all her friends and family nearby.

My dream for a happy life was not coming true. I painfully rediscovered that civilian life can have its own kind of threatening skies and stormy seas. My life's journey wasn't always smooth sailing as I had hoped for.

Much of my difficulties I brought upon myself. Over the years I dove into my work with such zeal that I had little time for my wife—and along the way, our four children. The business prospered and grew—and so did my ego! Remembering my childhood when the lack of money totally encompassed each day—and was probably the only source of arguments between my mother and father—I worked and worked and *worked*.

I thought I was completely in charge of my destiny—and don't get in my way! The war had hardened my heart against tragedy and dried up my emotions. I had little interest in people and no empathy for those with problems. My passion became the zeal to succeed and the desire to have money and personal recognition for success.

Yet the happiness I sought I could not find. All I received was dissatisfaction—with myself and life in general. My conversations were heavily peppered with profanity. Pressures were mounting, and my way of relaxing was to drink.

Because of my obsession with making something of myself in business, I neglected to give my wife Claire the love and affection she needed. She grew bitter and resentful for the years of my long hours at the office and so many days away on business trips. Her bitterness grew into rejection, which caused me to turn away from home life and throw myself into my work with even more determination. It was a vicious circle, and neither of us was willing to take the first step toward making our marriage work.

It was costly, ending in the early 1960s with three years of a haranguing divorce, and nothing to my credit. Adding to the emotional strain of that dark period in my life was the death of my Mother. Not long after my divorce, Claire remarried, only to die a few years later.

Meanwhile I was pursuing my life's goals to make money, attain high personal prestige, live in luxury and generally have a good time. The only responsibilities I wanted were those that bolstered my ego and satisfied my physical lusts. That meant running around with women, drinking, living high—doing whatever brought me personal pleasure.

# 24

# Searching Hearts

In 1974, after thirty years in the plastic injection molding business, I sold my company to the Carborundum Corporation and stayed on for three years under a working contract. I was particularly pleased with the arrangement because it allowed more time for me to live "the good life."

My fun-seeking lifestyle included considerable golf, and it was on the golf course in Woodstock, Vermont, where I met Susie Matthes who, unlike me, was a serious golfer. We were immediately attracted to one another, but she wanted nothing to do with my "eat, drink and be merry" philosophy. Before long we were together constantly and I abruptly quit running around with other women just to be with her. In fact, the more I was around her the more I settled down. Our feelings for each other deepened and, after about a year, we were married.

Since I had started a branch plant a few years earlier in Phoenix, Arizona, and Susie and I had come to enjoy the area, we elected to start our new life together there.

Susie, being a good athlete, quickly immersed herself in a new lifestyle of tennis and golf at the country club. My new diversions were investments and travel.

On the surface, we had everything anyone could ever want. We were very much in love with each other, were financially independent, lived in a beautiful house, had many friends, enjoyed good health and could travel whenever and wherever our hearts desired. In short, we enjoyed a comfortable life of leisure and pleasure.

As I said, *on the surface* we seemed to have it made. But deep inside, both of us—Susie more than I—felt that something important was missing in our lives...we did not know *what*!

Susie was searching for more meaning and fulfillment in life and decided she needed more responsibility and commitment outside our home. She returned to college where her diligence paid off with straight As. But, rewarding as that was, the restlessness came back. Simply accumulating knowledge did not remove the emptiness.

Then she tried a career as a travel agent. While a small weekly paycheck gave her a feeling of accomplishment, after three or four months the emptiness and anxiety returned.

She concluded that maybe she was just going through a stage in her life, and if she would ignore it and be patient, it would pass away.

Susie was not alone in her dilemma; I was feeling some of the same emptiness in my own life. I enjoyed dealing with investments and traveling, but something was definitely missing.

It was about that time that Susie began to sense that her problem might be religious in nature. This was interesting because we were already regularly attending a large Protestant church (mostly because I enjoyed listening to the choir).

Then the strangest thing happened: I found myself getting mad at the preacher because he did not teach about the Bible. He gave brilliant dissertations on social issues, theology and philosophy, but he sounded more like a college professor than a minister. Seldom did he mention Jesus Christ or quote the Bible. No one was jolted, no one was challenged. People were going to church because that is what you were supposed to do on Sunday morning.

For the first time in my life, I found myself wanting to understand the Bible. I had never before cared much about the Bible, so my new-found interest was puzzling.

Susie did not like that particular church, either, and went mostly to make me happy. I would ask her every Sunday after church about the minister's preaching: "Why doesn't he talk about the Bible? About God?" And whenever we were around others from the church, I expressed the same kind of negativism. I even threatened to leave the church. This went on for about a year, and still we made no effort to leave.

Sometimes, when Susie was feeling low, she even questioned whether she was a Christian, and I would reassure her that she was and so was I. After all, we attended church regularly, had been born into Christian families, were baptized, were morally good people, and did not doubt the existence of God and Jesus Christ. What else would a person have to do to be a better Christian?

New Year's Eve 1979 rolled around, and Susie made a resolution that would eventually change her life—and mine. We were at a country club with some friends, and everyone was making resolutions. Bud Neal, sitting next to my wife, said, "Susie, have you made your New Year's resolution?"

She hesitated for a moment, then, with a thoughtful smile answered, "Yes, Bud, I made my New Year's resolution: I'm going to be born again."

Susie's interjection of religion into this light-hearted conversation caused a little uneasiness and embarrassment which caught the rest of us off guard. Not knowing whether she was serious or joking, we responded with smiles and even some laughter—though not intended in any way to be condescending.

"No, I'm really serious," she insisted, explaining that she had seen how some born-again acquaintances seemed to have found real fulfillment and meaning in life. "So I'm going to be born again this year," she smiled, certain she was about to discover for herself some great secret to successful living.

The conversation quickly changed to another subject.

The cliche is that New Year's resolutions are made to be broken; but that was not the case with Susie. She fully intended to pursue her goal, and began attending another church with hopes of learning how to become born again.

This new church was affiliated with Susie's former denomination, which followed a liberal theology that did not subscribe to biblically conservative understanding of being born again. But this difference had to be learned by Susie. She started visiting the early morning worship service without me, then would come home, get me, and we would go to a service at our regular church. She even resorted to watching church programs on television, but still did not learn how to become born again. She just could not figure out what those so-called born-again people had that she did not have. All she knew was that the joy and peace they seemed to have was somehow tied to their being very religious people. Her conclusion was that she had to become more religious in order to be born again and to experience that same kind of outlook. What could she do to become more religious?

# 25

# Salvation for a Doomed Zoomie

It was not until early June that we saw a breakthrough. It came after a round of golf at the country club with a retired air force colonel and his wife, Al and Mary Lou Grimm. We had dinner with them afterwards, and this was an especially exciting opportunity for Susie, because she had heard they were born again.

She wasted no time in popping her questions: "Al, what does it mean to be born again? And how do you *get* born again? Because that's what I want, and I don't know how."

A warm understanding grin spread across Al's face. "It means," he said, "to be *spiritually* born."

Susie explained how she had started reading the Bible, hoping that would help her, but was having difficulty understanding it.

"Which version of the Bible?" he asked.

"The one I've had since I was twelve years old."

"Well, let me bring you another Bible—a modern translation which is easier to read. I think you'll be able to understand it."

The next day Al telephoned Susie to arrange to stop by our home and deliver her new Bible—as well as one for me. He asked if I would be there, too, and also if he could bring along a friend.

The date was set, and on Thursday Al arrived with his friend, Carl Combs, who is with Campus Crusade for Christ, a large inter-denominational evangelistic organization that began Bible studies on college campuses in the early 1950s and now sponsors evangelistic outreaches around the world. We went into our living room, and Al presented us with our Bibles. After a few minutes of casual conversation, Susie and I were handed a little booklet that Al said would help us understand what it means to be born again. On the booklet's cover was the question: "Have you ever heard of the Four Spiritual Laws?" Neither of us had.

Well, we started reading the booklet. The first spiritual law—or truth—was: "God Loves you and offers a wonderful plan for your life." Of course, this was backed up by some Bible verses. The first is probably the best-known verse in the Bible, John 3:16: "For God so loved the world, that He gave His only begotten Son, that whoever believes in Him should not perish, but have eternal life." Another verse was a quote by Jesus, in which He stated one of the purposes of His ministry: "I came that they might have life and have it abundantly" (John 10:10).

Al and Carl explained that those verses referred to the born again life—the spiritual birth that results from *knowing* Jesus Christ as Savior and Lord, in which one's life takes on a whole new, supernatural quality.

Suddenly, my mind was opening to what it meant to be a true Christian. All those years I had *believed* in God and Jesus Christ, but I never *knew* Christ as my personal Savior and Lord.

Then the second law brought into clearer focus that no matter how we might try to come to know God—through living

260

a good life, philosophy or some religion, the Bible says that man is sinful by nature and therefore separated from God. As a result, man, on his own, cannot know and experience God's love and plan for his life. "For the wages of sin is death," the booklet quoted Romans 6:23.

All this time, Susie thought she had to work harder at becoming more religious, and now we were hearing that good works and being religious were not the way to become born again—that is, to establish a personal relationship with Jesus Christ.

So then the logical question was: How *can* sinful man experience God's love and plan for his life? That, explained Carl, was answered by law three: Jesus Christ is the *only* way. Jesus, through His death on the cross, paid the penalty for man's sins, then He rose from the dead unto eternal life. Jesus promised that, if we *follow Him and believe in Him*, He will give us eternal life and bring us into fellowship with God (John 14:6).

That was exactly what Susie and I both wanted. Carl explained the fourth law: By receiving Jesus Christ by faith, as our Lord and Savior, we could become born again. From the little booklet, he read some verses to support what he said:

"But as many as received Him, to them He gave the right to become children of God, even to those who believe in His name" (John 1:12).

"For by grace you have been saved through faith; and that not of yourselves, it is the gift of God; not as a result of works, that no one should boast" (Ephesians 2:8, 9).

Carl read John 3:1-8 from his Bible, which explains that in order for us to have a relationship with God we must be spiritually born.

*Receive Him? Saved through faith? The gift of God, not of works? Be born again?* As I listened and thought, I experienced the exhilerating awareness deep within my soul that I was on the brink of discovering something very truthful and very spiritually profound. I had always believed in Jesus Christ and God, and was taught to like most people. But I didn't *know* Christ! Now I was beginning to see that attending church regularly did not make me a Christian, neither was being born into a Christian family nor being baptized nor being a morally good person nor simply believing in the existence of God or knowing *about* Jesus Christ.

It was all beginning to make sense—except for one thing: *How* do you become born again?

Carl turned in the booklet and read a quote of Jesus from the Book of Revelation: "Behold, I stand at the door and knock; if anyone hears my voice and opens the door, I will come into him" (Rev. 3:20). He interpreted the passage to mean that Jesus has been standing at the door of my life, knocking, wanting to come in and fellowship with me. Wow! In my case Jesus had been standing there knocking for a long time!

He was knocking when my mother first told me about Him when I was a little kid.

He was knocking when I rose out of a near-poverty family background to attend college.

He was knocking when persecution had to be overcome to get into the Navy.

He was knocking when I got shot down.

He was knocking when I crashed into the tail of my Hellcat.

He was knocking when my chute popped open at low altitude.

He was knocking when the chute dragged me, half paralyzed, through the rough sea.

He was knocking when those sharks did not attack.

He was knocking when the wind and tide and current carried me to that island.

He was knocking when Sam Dealey rescued me, when the *Harder* survived that near fatal dive and when that torpedo missed the sub.

He was knocking when I flew all those remaining combat missions, when my guns jammed and caused me to duck out of the way of that Jap shell.

He was knocking in all the years that followed—through a failed marriage, through business successes, through meeting and marrying Susie, and through all sorts of good and bad times.

Throughout all those years He was knocking at the door of my life, and I kept ignoring Him. Well, I no longer could ignore His knocking; it was finally time to open the door of my life to Him.

"Would you like to receive Christ right now?" Carl asked Susie and me, almost as if he could read our minds.

"Yes!" exclaimed Susie. And I, with a broad grin, nodded my head in agreement! Carl invited us to talk to God directly about it by praying the suggested prayer at the back of the *Four Spiritual Laws* booklet. He read the prayer and pointed out that God is more concerned with the attitude of our heart than He is with our words.

"Does this prayer express the desires of your hearts?" asked Carl. Susie and I agreed that it did and Carl led us as we prayed out loud:

"Lord Jesus, I need You. Thank You for dying on the cross for my sins. I open the door of my life and receive You as my Savior and Lord. Thank You for forgiving my sins and giving me eternal life. Take control of the throne of my life. Make me the kind of person You want me to be."[1]

Susie was surprised that I said the prayer too, because she did not know that I was interested in becoming born again; and I honestly did not know I was either!

After Carl and Al left the house, I turned to Susie and said, "Hey, he says we are born-again Christians!"

"Do you feel any different?" Susie asked.

"Nope," I answered, "Do you?"

"No, but as Al said, we have a lot of growing to do now."

# 26

# Clearer Skies and Calmer Seas

The next morning, I was awake before Susie and went into the garden with a cup of coffee—and, of all things, the Bible! After more than two years of dissatisfaction with the non-biblical sermons I had been hearing, Susie's remark the night before had made me realize that in all that time I had never read the Bible for myself. So I sat down with my coffee and started to read.

Minutes later, Susie awakened, found the bed empty next to her, and wandered outsided, only to discover what I was doing.

"I don't believe it!" she exclaimed with a smile of approval.

"You know," I responded, rather nonchalantly, "the Bible's kind of interesting."

That prompted Susie to start reading the Bible. And where do you start? Right at the beginning, she reasoned—with the Book of Genesis. But two weeks and several pages later, she was ready to give up.

John and Susie Galvin

She talked to Al about it, and he suggested that we begin reading the Bible starting with the Book of John. We did, and suddenly the Bible started to come alive for us! It was almost as if each page we read was written just to answer our questions.

We began to be aware of other Christians around us—people who had similar yearnings to know more about the Bible and Jesus Christ. We started attending a church where the teaching was centered on the Bible. No fruitless philosophy, no hammering out humanism—nothing but the truth of God's word!

We both joined Bible studies, continued to study the Bible on our own and took every opportunity to talk with other Christians about Jesus and the Bible.

And then, gradually, the inner peace and joy and contentment that Susie had wanted started to take hold in her life...and in mine. No longer was I striving to prove something to myself or to anyone else. I was learning how to be at peace with myself, with the world, and with God.

For years, thinking back on my close calls with death, I had asked, "Why me?" Why was my life spared? Why was I saved when others died? Knowing that Death is inevitable sometimes tempers the harsh reality of coping when the life of someone near us is lost. Nevertheless, we are prone to view some death from a human perspective as being unnecessary or premature. Our hurt can turn into anger and resentfulness. Sometimes this leads to blaming God for unjustly permitting the death and to doubt His love.

The truth is that God is *not* our enemy—*sin* is our enemy, and as a result of our inherent sin nature, we are born spiritually dead and mortally dying. The beautiful thing that God has done, out of His love for us, is to provide a way of salvation through His Son, Jesus Christ, who conquered sin and death. Jesus died on the cross to pay the penalty for our sins. He overcame death and was resurrected on the third day.

All we have to do is accept that forgiveness by faith. When we do, we become children of God and receive new spiritual life that is eternal (1 John 5:11-15). This is what Jesus refers to in the third chapter of John when He says that each of us needs to be spiritually born.

Of course we still walk around in mortal bodies that are suseptible to sin and death. But when Jesus returns He will give us new bodies that are impervious to sin and death (1 Corinthians 15), and we will spend eternity with Him!

Meanwhile, Jesus provides a way through His Holy Spirit for us to enjoy a life of purpose and meaning. This comes to us through our faith and obedience, and we are obedient because we trust Him—in all circumstances, even the "untimely" death of someone close to us.

I no longer ask God *why* He saved my life and allowed others to lose their's, but rather *what* He wants me to do with my life until that day when I go to be with Him. While I do not have all the answers yet, as I study God's word each day and look to Him for strength and guidance, I gain more and more understanding of His plan for my life.

In years past, everything had centered around myself, with little regard for anyone else. But now my life is more Christ-centered than John-centered. I stopped using profanity—and I mean stopped cold! I am learning how to trust God in coping with life's problems and no longer look to the bottle for escape. I am seeing life—and people—from a new perspective. I find other people interesting. I am discovering that God gives beautiful meaning and purpose to life (a realization that has changed my cynicism into optimism). The fulfillment I sought but never found through lustful desires, money, possessions and social status, I am now experiencing through a deep desire to follow Christ and to love others unconditionally. I have been shown a whole new quality of life with more fulfilling values. These are becoming real to me—as a result of what Christ is doing in and through me!

Jesus said, "I came that you might have life and have it abundantly." I can tell you now that I have tasted that spiritually abundant life, and that I look forward to tomorrow and what God has further planned for me with an enthusiasm I have never known before!

Now before you write me off as a self-righteous super-saint, let me make it clear that I certainly have not arrived yet. I have only begun to grow spiritually and have a long way to go! But as I experience more of the better way God has for me, the less I *desire* to sin. Each day as I read the Bible I am reminded that God loves me, that my sins are forgiven, that I can look forward to eternal life with my Heavenly Father, and that God, through His Holy Spirit, wants to help me live a life of meaning and fulfillment.

Today I know that God sent Sam Dealy to save my life and that He sent His Son, Jesus Christ, to save my soul. He also sent Susie, not only as my wife, but also to be the instrument to help lead me to Jesus Christ. Even after so many years of my old kind of life, it was not too late!

Well now you know my story. That morning when I sat up in bed, it was just as if someone had said, "John, you'd better get to work! Go tell the story of your life. And go tell about *Me*." This, then, is what He wants me to do—share my new life in Christ with others—by telling them about the love and forgiveness of His Son and by helping them realize their potential as children of God. And that is my purpose in writing this book.

Now let us focus on *you* for a moment: Look back over the years of your own life: There surely have been times when Jesus Christ was knocking on the door of *your* life. Perhaps you did not hear, or maybe—like me for too many years—you ignored it. Well, it is not too late for you to open that door of your life to Jesus Christ. Read this chapter again, particularly the pages dealing with the *Four Spiritual Laws*. Then pray that little prayer and by faith receive Jesus Christ as your Savior and Lord. As He promised in Revelation 3:20, *He will come in!*

If you prayed that prayer by faith to invite Christ into your life, or if you want to know more about becoming a Christian or how to live a more rewarding Christian life, I invite you to write to me and I will send you some helpful literature—free and without any obligation on your part. My address is:

John Galvin
P.O. Box 5745
Scottsdale AZ 85261.

I look forward to hearing from you.

About the authors...

**John Galvin** returned to combat and became an ace credited with seven enemy aircraft, two assists and a 6000-ton transport. He was awarded four Distinquished Flying Crosses, several Air Medals, Purple Heart, Submarine Combat Award and two Presidential Unit Citations (while serving aboard the U.S.S. *Bunker Hill* and the U.S.S. *Harder*).

After the war Galvin passionately threw himself into building a successful plastics business. Years later he turned to investments and travel. Today he and his wife Susie live in Scottsdale, Arizona and give much of themselves to evangelististic work.

**Frank Allnutt,** formerly a Navy parachute rigger, has spent the last eighteen-years in publishing, television and marketing, with a stint as public relations manager for WED (Walt E. Disney) Enterprises. He has authored ten books, including three inspirational bestsellers: *The Force of Star Wars, After The Omen* and a novel, *The Peacemaker.*

# Notes

CHAPTER 9
[1]Lockwood, V. Adm. Charles A, *Through Hell and Deep Water*, (NY: Greenberg: Publisher, 1956), pp230, 231.

CHAPTER 11
[1]*Through Hell and Deep Water*, p237.
[2]*Ibid*, pp237-8.
[3]*Ibid*, pp238-9.
[4]*Ibid*, pp239.

CHAPTER 12
[1]*Information Bulletin*, Bureau of Naval Personnel, April 1945, p16.
[2]"Hit 'em Again, Harder," *The Blue Book*, June 1949.
[3]Log of the U.S.S. *Harder*, April 1, 1944.
[4]*Through Hell and Deep Water*, pp240-1.
[5]*Ibid*, p241.

CHAPTER 15
[1]*Through Hell and Deep Water*, p248.
[2]*Ibid*. pp248-91.

CHAPTER 16
[1]*Through Hell and Deep Water*, p253.
[2]Log of the U.S.S. *Harder*.
[3]*Through Hell and Deep Water*, p253.

CHAPTER 17
[1]*Through Hell and Deep Water*, p254.
[2]Log of the U.S.S. *Harder*, April 16, 1944.
[3]*Ibid*.
[4]*Ibid*.
[5]*Through Hell and Deep Water*, pp261-3.

CHAPTER 21
[1]"Hit 'em Again, *Harder!*" *Blue Book* magazine, June 1949, p30.

CHAPTER 25
[1]*Have You Heard of the Four Spiritual Laws?* (Campus Crusade for Christ International: San Bernardino, Calif.), p10.